W9-AQW-261

THE WALL
STREET

DATE DUE

JAN 1 0 2015			
APR 0 6 2016			
NO 2 5 '17			

Demco, Inc. 38-293

THE WALL STREET JOURNAL.

COMPLETE HOME OWNER'S GUIDEBOOK

Make the Most of Your
Biggest Asset in Any Market

DAVID CROOK

THREE RIVERS PRESS
NEW YORK

South Burlington Community Library
540 Dorset Street
~~~~~~~~~~ ~~ ~~~~~

Published in the United States by Three Rivers Press, an imprint of the
Crown Publishing Group, a division of Random House, Inc., New York.
www.crownpublishing.com

Three Rivers Press and the Tugboat design are registered trademarks of
Random House, Inc.

The Wall Street Journal ® is a registered trademark of Dow Jones and is used by
permission.

Grateful acknowledgment is made to the following for permission to use
photographs/illustrations: p. 45, © Val Bochkov c/o theispot.com; p. 50,
© Richard Downs c/o theispot.com; p. 69, © Jose Ortega c/o theispot.com;
p. 84, © Phil Bliss c/o theispot.com; p. 108, © Steven Salerno c/o theispot.com;
p. 134, © Michael Austin c/o theispot.com; p. 142, © Robert Dale c/o
theispot.com; p. 152, © Phil Foster c/o theispot.com; p. 160, © Hal Mayforth
c/o theispot.com; p. 179, © Douglas Jones c/o theispot.com; p. 198, © Robert
Saunders c/o theispot.com.

Library of Congress Cataloging-in-Publication Data

Crook, David, 1953–
The Wall Street Journal complete home owner's guidebook : make the most
of your biggest asset in any market / David Crook.—1st ed.
    p. cm.
Includes bibliographical references and index.
1. House buying—Costs.   2. Home ownership—Costs.   3. Real-estate
investment.   I. Title.   II. Title: Complete home owner's guidebook.
HD1379.C76 2008
643'.12—dc22   2008025355

ISBN 978-0-307-40592-0

Printed in the United States of America

Design by Mauna Eichner and Lee Fukui

10 9 8 7 6 5 4 3 2 1

First Edition

CONTENTS

THE WALL STREET JOURNAL.

COMPLETE HOME OWNER'S GUIDEBOOK

INTRODUCTION
YOUR BIGGEST ASSET

I have an expensive hobby: buying homes,
redoing them, tearing them down and building
them up the way they want to be built.

— SANDRA BULLOCK

This book is about big dreams and the money it takes to achieve them.

Above all, it's about buying and owning your own home, which, to most of us, is the foundation of the American Dream of freedom and prosperity.

For the vast majority of home-owning Americans, our houses are our largest assets—often representing hundreds of thousands of dollars of family wealth and most, if not all, of our net worth. But few of us know how to manage these huge assets. That's because from a financial point of view, most of our ideas about home buying, owning and selling are distorted, ambiguous and, often, flat-out wrong.

We listen to our home-owning parents, friends and co-workers tell tales of effortless wealth building; it seems they all cracked the mystery of making lots and lots of money by buying a house way back when and then selling right at the top of the market: "Do nothing but live in the place and then cash out." What could be easier?

Worse yet, we listen to the promises of the home-owning industry, real-estate and home-improvement hawkers whose financial interests are usually at considerable odds with our own. What they tell us boils down to this: "Spend. Spend. Spend. Buy more house. Buy farther out into the suburbs. Remodel the kitchen. Put in a pool." On and on and on.

Yes, owning your own home is a wonderful feeling. There are few moments in life more sublime than when the moving van pulls away and it hits you—this new home is *yours*. Whether it's a cramped apartment in Manhattan or a mid-century ranch in the San Fernando Valley, a home of your own is the cornerstone in the American ideal of personal accomplishment and independence.

But what are the real costs of home ownership?

Far more than you think.

For starters, home owning makes a huge claim on the finances of individuals, made all the worse as home values throughout the country have fallen in the past few years. The situation was bad enough in 2006, just as the collapse of the real-estate bubble was becoming apparent. Back then, according to the Federal Reserve, half the value of all Americans' homes was mortgaged. Put another way: for every dollar that Americans had invested in their homes, 50 cents was borrowed money. And that was in a boom! In the housing depression we're now experiencing in much of the country, overall values have fallen so far that many "owners" actually owe more money on their houses than they could get selling them. To put it in the same language: for every dollar of home, $1.25 is borrowed money.

Throughout this book, I'm going to use the word *home-owner* sparingly, and not just because it's a clunky coinage that would be better expressed with two words, *home owner*. No, I'm going to avoid it where I can because most people living in their own homes are not really home owners at all. They're home *buyers*. The important distinction being made is that a home buyer is someone still in the process of purchasing his or her home, and it takes most of us many, many years to do that.

This is not just word play, but an effort to refocus your thinking, to get you to appreciate that the process of becoming a home owner is a long-term, active financial exercise that begins only in the three or four months it takes to find a house, get a mortgage, hire movers, sign the closing papers and get in the door. That wonderful moment when the moving van pulls away is just one early step in a lifelong process of building your wealth. If you think of a home owner as someone who has just finished a marathon, that moment when you wave good-bye to the movers is more like the first time your parents let you walk to the end of the block by yourself.

Owning your own home is a reward for wisely managing your life and money and building financial security. It's not a way to achieve it.

For most Americans it takes about thirty years from the day you move in, sometime in your late twenties or early thirties, to reach full-fledged home ownership. Some start the cycle earlier, some later. Some are mortgage free in their early fifties; others are still making house payments into their seventies.

Along the way, your interests as a buyer-owner will change as you age and your family circumstances, job and life change. For example, the concerns of a young couple struggling to

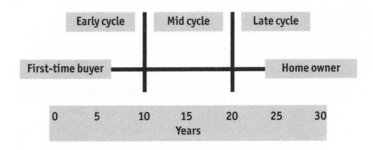

make their payments on a condo are far different from those of a middle-aged couple with two teenagers and just one bathroom or those of a widow alone in a five-bedroom house.

This book is structured to parallel those stages of home buying, from your initial decision to buy a house through full ownership. I've divided the entire process into three ten-year periods, the early-, mid- and late-years of the "thirty-year home-buying cycle," which doesn't actually come to an end until you have paid off your mortgage debt. That's when you become an actual home owner.

Keep in mind: This thirty-year cycle is not science, nor does it pertain to the buying of just one house. Most Americans move up two, three or more times over their home-buying years, rolling their equity from one house into the next and the next. So think of the long-term cycle as the period that people are actively in the home-buying process, or, as it's more often put, "in the housing market."

INVESTMENTS AND ASSETS

Let's get some general terminology straight. All through this book, you'll see homes referred to as "assets" but not always as "investments." That's a distinction and a difference.

All investments are assets but not all assets are investments. When you make an investment, you buy it expecting to receive income while you hold it, a profit when you sell it or both. An asset is anything you can convert to cash, either by selling it or offering it as collateral for a loan.

Liquid assets, like stocks, can be converted to cash quickly; hard assets, like a car, take time.

Here's another way to look at it: The $1,000 loan you make to your cousin at 8% interest for three years is an investment. The electric guitar he buys with it is an asset that he can turn into $100 if he hocks it at a pawnshop.

A home is a bit of both, certainly a big, hard asset and, for readers of this book, a smart investment.

AFTER THE BUBBLE

There's a saying in the real-estate business: "If you think you own your house, stop making your payments and see what happens."

Tens of thousands of Americans are learning that lesson the hard way: they are losing their homes. With the foreclosure notices go their savings, their peace of mind, their images of themselves as participants in the nation's great wealth-producing machine. Their dreams are being tossed out on the curb with the furniture.

But it didn't have to be that way.

In the first few years of the new century, Americans' long fixation with home owning metastasized into the biggest residential real-estate bubble in history. Meanwhile, the home-owning cultural mania prevailed twenty-four hours a day on cable-TV networks such as HGTV, Fine Living and The Learning Channel, at every Home Depot and Lowe's in every suburb in the country, on newsstands where there was a magazine for every taste and house style (from *Country Living* to *Wallpaper,* from *Old House Journal* to *Dwell*). All telling you that every dollar you spend on your home is worth more than a dollar in the bank or in government bonds or in the stock market or just about anywhere else you could put it. Home owning, went much of the bubble era's conventional wisdom, was the one financial sure thing.

Get real. Home owning is not now, was not then and never has been a guaranteed moneymaker. Ask anyone who sold a house in Texas in the 1980s . . . or southern California in the early 1990s . . . or most recently in Las Vegas, San Diego, Phoenix, Miami, Tampa or any number of other deflated bubble markets of the Sun Belt. Ask owners in Kansas City who can look only longingly at the long-term price appreciation enjoyed by their home-owning peers on the coasts. Ask anyone in the former industrial centers of the Midwest or the working towns of New England if they got rich on their houses.

That's not to say, of course, that home owning didn't look and often act like a sure thing through much of the last half of the twentieth century. But now, as the nation shakes off the hangover of the most recent real-estate mania, home owning is changing dramatically. There is every reason to believe that the high-water mark of American home owning has been hit and is now falling back. At the height of the bubble, nearly 70% of American families owned their own homes, with the last couple of percentage points coming from a wave of financially marginal buyers who are now struggling to hold on to their houses or have already lost them.

Speculators, who in some areas powered as much as 40% of the home-buying orgy, have bailed. Already on the horizon: the first of millions of Baby Boomers who are looking to cash out, with many of them hoping to fund all or part of twenty- or thirty-year retirements with the money they'll get selling their homes. That's a lot of supply, and the demand for all those houses is, at best, iffy.

And as bad as things were immediately after the late-2005 peak of the housing bubble, no one was prepared for the breakdown of the financial system in the late summer of 2008. Like an out-of-control nuclear chain reaction, the housing debacle slammed through the banking system. What began as a wave of home-loan defaults among bad-risk "sub-prime" borrowers exploded into a global financial crisis like nothing anyone has seen since the Great Depression of the 1930s.

The financial fission reached critical mass in a two-week frenzy as the U.S. government rapidly nationalized Fannie Mae, Freddie Mac and American International Group (the nation's two largest mortgage guarantors and the largest insurer of mortgage-backed securities) and launched a $1 trillion program to assume the country's most troubled mortgage debts.

That was just the climax of the crisis; the resolution has yet to come. The U.S. economy is facing a period of profound uncertainty. No one has been on this road before, and no one knows how all of this is going to play out.

This much we know: The dollar is struggling. Oil is consuming larger and larger portions of the nation's income. Ven-

erable financial institutions have gone bankrupt or sold themselves off at yard-sale prices. Business credit is tight. And home
mortgages are more and more difficult to obtain.

None of that bodes well for a home-buying economy that
relies ultimately on the twin pillars of prosperity: easy borrowing and new jobs. For much of the country, that means
home values are unlikely to continue going up as they did for
the first half of the decade and, as we have already seen in
many places, will actually decline. Indeed, for the first time
since records have been kept, the median home price in the
United States actually fell in 2007 and continued to fall
through 2008. It is widely believed in investment circles that
the housing market will continue suffering for years to come.

Yale economist Robert Shiller—regarded with his partner
Karl Case of Wellesley College as the nation's top student of
the housing market—predicts that the downturn could last far
into the next decade, as the vanguard of the retiring Baby
Boomers head toward their seventies.

When more and more Americans are relying on their
homes as the foundations of their financial planning, such a
prolonged chill on home prices could be devastating.

Buyers, owners and sellers need to prepare themselves for
this new, uncertain era. In this book, I'll show you—whether
you are a young adult looking to buy a first home, a family hoping to move up to a dream home or an empty nester cashing
out—how to make the most of your biggest asset.

We will look at the financial issues facing Baby Boomers,
who are trying to maximize the gains they have in their homes,
as well as the plans of Generation Xers, who are now in their
prime home-buying years, and Generation Yers, who are just
now entering the workforce.

You'll see:

- Why your home isn't the investment you think it is

- Why you shouldn't buy more house than you can
  comfortably afford

- Why the bigger house isn't always the best house

- Why you shouldn't spend so much improving your house

- Why so many home-owning costs are hidden or ignored by home owners

- Why you don't make the kind of profits on homes that you expect

In short, then, we'll examine traditional real-estate wisdom and find a lot of it lacking. We'll learn how some conventional "dos" of home buying will cost plenty of money, while some of the "don'ts" might make plenty. We will look at why some people buy houses when they shouldn't, and why most people don't make nearly as much selling a house as they think they do.

In many ways, it's easier to say what you should not expect from this book than what you should. This is not about how to buy a house, though there is a lot of that in it. Nor is this book about how to sell a house, though there is some of that, too. What this book is mainly about is the period in between. It's about the decades, the lifetimes even, that we spend living in our biggest financial assets without understanding how to manage them.

There are no secret home-owning schemes here, no special tips that aren't readily apparent to anyone who understands the basics of finance and management. And there are no guaranteed moneymaking strategies that are beyond the skills of someone who can wield a paintbrush or a hammer.

What there are a lot of, however, are warnings and "hey, wait a minute" moments, in which I raise questions about some bit of conventional home-owning wisdom. At the same time, I'll try to show you how to approach home buying from a more realistic and financially prudent point of view.

SEVEN KEYS TO SMART HOME OWNING

1. **Think differently.** It's a house—not a savings account, not an investment fund, not a retirement nest egg. Recognize your house for what it really is—an expensive installment-plan purchase that promises you a hefty rebate down the line. The best way to make a true profit on a home is to pay as little for it as you can. That means buy cheaper and buy quicker. Your goal should always be to buy a home significantly below— 20%, 30%, 40% below—the prices for similar properties and to pay for it in much fewer than the standard thirty years.

2. **Learn the difference between wants and needs.** Housing is a necessity, but there are very few people who can honestly claim they need six bedrooms or a master suite a quarter the size of a basketball court. What you *have* to have in a home is a good structure in a good neighborhood. That's worth whatever you have to pay. Anything beyond that, however, is what you *want* to have. And the costs of what you want in your home should be weighed against all the other needs and wants of your life.

3. **Add up *all* the costs of a home.** There's much more to buying and owning a home than just the monthly payments. There are insurance, property taxes, yard maintenance, home owner's association fees and other bills directly related to the house. Then there are the costs that are not immediately associated with home owning but are the result of it nonetheless— the extra furniture for the extra bedrooms, the pool service, the third car you buy because your neighborhood has no public transit and your teenager goes to a high school on the other side of town or the extra gasoline you must buy because you work twenty-five miles away. On top of those kinds of out-of-pocket expenses, there are other intangible costs: What's a two-hour commute each way worth if it means you leave most mornings before the kids get up and you come home after they've gone to bed? Is a full-time babysitter worth the cost of you and your husband working full-time jobs just to afford a mortgage payment?

4. **Control your biggest expense.** Speed up your loan repayments. A typical home bought with a mortgage today will end up costing its buyer $1

million over the next thirty years. The first way to significantly cut that cost is to reduce interest costs by accelerating your principal payments. Caution: don't defer retirement savings in favor of rapid mortgage payments. Do both.

5. **Share the burden.** Buy a two-family house or a multi-family building or even just a house with a rental unit as your first home. Pay it off quickly, bulking up your monthly payments with your tenants' rent and paying off your mortgage early. Then use that house to buy your dream home. You will get out of debt more quickly, have more money to pay for your new home, save more in your retirement fund and use less of your regular income for future housing costs.

6. **Watch the renovating.** Build a new kitchen—or bath or bedroom—because you want it or need it, not because it will make you a profit or enhance the value of your home. A top-of-the-line kitchen remodel like you see on TV or in shelter magazines will cost you more than $100,000 and repay only about 76%. Borrow the money, and your loss will be worse. If you must remodel, pay cash. Do whatever work you can yourself, and you will see huge savings.

7. **Don't move so often.** Staying put is the best way to build equity, especially in an era when you can't count on rising values. Most Americans stay in their homes only about seven years, and end up paying four times in interest what they have paid on their loan balance. Then they buy a new house and start the mortgage clock all over again. Stay put and build your equity the old-fashioned way—by paying down your principal.

We'll delve into the seven points of smart home owning throughout the book. Chapter 1, **"Why in the World Do You Want a House?,"** explores the most familiar financial arguments for buying a home and finds most of them wanting in a post-bubble world. In chapter 2, **"Home Owning in a Troubled Market,"** we look at the impact of today's housing market at various points along the home-buying cycle and offer specific advice for wherever you are in the cycle. It's great to be a first-time buyer today, but current actual home owners could be facing some tough times.

Chapter 3, **"Managing Your Biggest Debt,"** introduces the idea that in home owning managing your biggest asset is really all about managing the loan or loans that you have taken out to buy it. We follow that up in chapter 4 with **"Making Your Debt Work for You,"** which looks at smart ways to borrow against the equity that you have in your home.

We start in on the main topics of the home-buying cycle in chapter 5, **"How to Buy a Home,"** which focuses on first-time and early-cycle buyers, and looks specifically at opportunities they face getting set on the course of owning a home. Chapter 6, **"Settling In,"** focuses on the decisions facing mid-cycle home buyers who may be feeling cramped by their current home or are longing for a move up to a bigger house in another part of town. And in chapter 7, **"Free and Clear,"** we talk about how late-cycle and actual home owners can fit their biggest asset into retirement and estate planning.

Finally, in chapter 8, **"The Pursuit of Happiness,"** we'll recap the big points and finish with a flourish on achieving your dreams and building a legacy without going broke in the process.

That's the end. But now, let's start at the beginning, with the first question anyone reading this book needs to ask. . . .

CHAPTER 1

Why in the World Do You Want a House?

The house came to be haunted by the unspoken phrase:
'There must be more money! There must be more money!'
— D. H. Lawrence

Most people think of their homes as savings accounts that they live in. They figure their home is the perfect "two-fer" deal: the expense of owning a house is the "rent"—what they have to pay for the cost of shelter—while their gradually accumulating equity and appreciation build a nest egg they can tap someday to send the kids to college, fund their retirements or take a trip to Disney World.

Sounds like a sure thing, making money as you pay for one of life's necessities.

Don't bet the house on it; that nest egg has a big crack in it. That's because houses are not very good investment vehicles. Economic studies have demonstrated over and over that houses actually cost more to buy and live in than most people make when they sell them. In fact, they rarely match the long-term returns of stocks or other investments.

RESIDENTIAL REAL ESTATE VERSUS OTHER INVESTMENTS (1987–2007)

	After inflation return (annual)
Single-family homes*	–.06%
Large-cap stocks	6.63%
Small-cap stocks	6.34%
International stocks	3.01%
Municipal bonds	4.01%
Long-term government bonds	2.94%
Corporate bonds	1.48%
Intermediate government bonds	1.31%

Note: Price appreciation only; data provided by Winan's International.
© 2008 Thornburg Investment Management, Inc.

Why such a poor showing? Houses cost a lot to own and operate, with monthly payments and related expenses typically eating up more than one-third of a young family's income at a time when they could be saving more efficiently for college or old age.

That's not even addressing the common practice of borrowing against home equity to spend money on things with no investment value at all, such as paying off credit cards or buying cars, boats or vacations. There's nothing quite as stupid as finally paying for your 2007 trip to Orlando in 2037, when you settle up your refinanced "cash-out" thirty-year mortgage.

All of this is doubly true today, with much of the country in a real-estate depression. It's unlikely that cash-strapped, house-poor home owners will be bailed out by a new wave of rising prices anytime soon. Like 1990s tech-stock buyers still waiting for the Nasdaq to recover, many of today's owners could be stuck in their homes for years and years with little chance of appreciating values contributing to the sizeable bonus equity that they hoped for and, unfortunately, may have counted on.

"Real-estate investments suffer serious and sometimes prolonged downturns," says economist W. Van Harlow in an early

2007 study of home equity and retirement from the Fidelity Research Institute in Boston. "A real-estate 'bust' could be quite damaging to an investor nearing retirement who relied too heavily on home equity."

Keep that in mind as you read this chapter's question-and-answer rundown of some of the big financial issues facing home buyers and home owners. These issues and problems will be discussed much more fully in later chapters.

Q: My home is my largest asset. Why shouldn't I rely on it as the cornerstone of financial planning?

A: Because a house can be an inefficient means of investing, and it costs far more to buy and operate than you think. Home owners can easily end up paying more to live in their houses than the supposed "profit" they make when they sell them.

When most home owners figure their returns, they don't do much more than subtract the price they paid from the price they received. Then they come up with a really big return because they paid only a 5% or 10% down payment. So they figure they made a huge "profit."

But they didn't. That's because the costs of owning a home—buying it with a long-term mortgage and then paying taxes on it, insuring it, repairing it, renovating it—sap most of what most home owners think they make in price appreciation.

Houses are nice financially because you and your family have to have shelter, and there are not many other things you buy that actually go up in value and can put a six-figure check in your pocket when you sell them. But don't delude yourself: you've probably already spent most of that check, and you'll spend whatever's left in just a few days when you buy a new home.

Think of your sale proceeds another way: not as a true profit, but as a large *rebate*. Some of the thousands of dollars that you paid into the house over the years are being returned to you—sometimes with a bonus, often without.

Q: BUT I'VE ALWAYS HEARD THAT BUYING A HOUSE IS THE BEST INVESTMENT I'LL EVER MAKE!

A: That says more about the investor than the investment. Do you suppose that the best investment Warren Buffett ever made was his house?

Here's a chart that compares thirty years of home appreciation with thirty years of the Dow Jones Industrial Average, the most widely cited stock-market indicator. As you can see, it's no contest, even during the huge home-price run-ups of the last ten years.

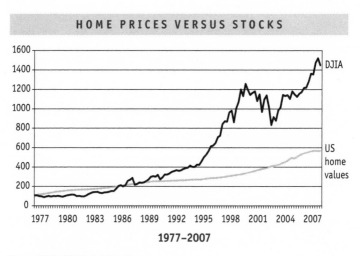

HOME PRICES VERSUS STOCKS

1977–2007

Source: OFHEO, WSJ Markets Data Group.

For a long time, buying a house was about the only investment easily accessible and affordable to the middle class. Although there are many more opportunities to invest today— discount brokers, 401(k) plans, mutual funds and so forth— and fully half of the nation's households own stocks, very few Americans still have much in the way of financial assets.

Excluding real estate, the median net worth of Americans is just about $28,000.

Grappling with consumer debts, car payments, health-care costs, rising gasoline prices and all their other expenses, much of the middle class can't afford to invest anything in the future when they are so hard-pressed in the present. So when they do get a bit ahead, they often end up spending what little investment money they have on a home. Given their circumstances and choices, a house probably *is* the best investment most Americans will ever make.

But don't brag about it.

Q: But isn't it always better to buy a house than to rent? Rent just goes up and up every year, but a house payment stays the same forever!

A: Yes, rents do rise. But so do home owners' costs. If you have a fixed-rate mortgage, your monthly loan payment will stay the same but all your other costs—property taxes, association fees, utilities—will rise right alongside the renter's costs. Stay in one house for many years, and your house note could well be your cheapest monthly expense.

As to whether it's *always* better to buy than rent, that depends on when and where you buy, and how long you own. Buy at the wrong time—like during the bubble, or in Texas in the 1980s—and you could well end up wishing you had rented instead.

Boom market or bust, home buying has so many extra costs—from upfront "points" paid to a lender to title insurance and appraisal fees, from the huge monthly interest payment to monthly maintenance or home owner association fees—that over the first five to seven years, a renter who invests the equivalent of a down payment in stocks could easily do better overall than a house buyer. Compounding that problem: most home owners move within just seven years!

As the ownership timeline stretches out to fifteen, twenty or thirty years, however, post–World War II history indicates that the buyer will almost certainly do better than the renter in the long term. Well-maintained houses in good neighborhoods generally *do* appreciate in value, at least as much as inflation. The government subsidizes home buyers' mortgage-interest payments with a tax deduction, and married couples get a delightful no-tax-at-all break on the first $500,000 of profit they make when they sell. The benefits of those tax breaks are oversold—they aren't nearly as generous as most home buyers think—but they are still much better than what renters get.

The typical buy-versus-rent argument clouds a more important point that affects far more people, though: a house is a mediocre way to build wealth.

The important issue for home buyers and owners shouldn't be whether to buy or rent; it's how much to invest in a house versus stocks, bonds, investment properties or other things. Far too many Americans spend too much on their houses, missing out on the better returns of other investments.

And that especially stings at retirement time, when many home owners plan to sell, take their profits, buy another home in a cheaper locale and bank the rest.

That is the essence of a speculative bubble: it depends on a greater fool coming along, willing to pay you a whole lot more for your home than you paid for it. That's a scenario that may not be repeated in the United States for a long while.

Q: STILL, EVEN IF THERE ISN'T A LOT OF APPRECIATION, ISN'T IT BETTER TO BE MAKING MORTGAGE PAYMENTS AND BUILDING EQUITY THAN PAYING RENT?

A: Buying a house with a long-term mortgage is just another form of renting. Mortgage interest is rent that you pay to your lender for the use of its money rather than to a landlord for the use of his house.

Because the government believes that it's a net social benefit to the country to have a lot of home buyers, it subsidizes the interest portion of a monthly mortgage payment with a tax deduction. Years ago, that was a pretty good deal, but now the benefits of the mortgage deduction are way overblown.

Q: Isn't that the best thing going for home owners? The government doesn't help renters.

A: Well actually, every renter in the country gets a hefty tax deduction every year. It's called the standard deduction and it's gradually becoming more valuable than the mortgage-interest deduction.

Yes, the mortgage-interest deduction is just about the only additional tax break left to middle-class, salaried taxpayers. But for most of us it's nothing to write home about. It's a tax subsidy that recaptures only a small portion of the real costs of borrowing to buy a moderately priced home and living in it. And as taxpayers' standard deduction keeps going up year by year, the mortgage-interest deduction is quietly disappearing for all but the wealthiest of home buyers and those buying more expensive houses.

To see how little value the home-buyer's deduction actually has, look at the difference between the ways the government taxes two different types of property owners, home owners and landlords.

They might even be neighbors with houses next door to each other. Bob is a landlord who invests in a house that he rents to someone else; he is far better off on April 15 than Bill, a home owner who lives in his "investment."

That's because Bob writes off, dollar for dollar, the property's expenses against its income and pays tax on only the difference between his costs of owning and the rents he receives. If he rents a house for $2,500 a month and it costs him $2,000 to operate—to pay his mortgage, property taxes, maintenance, utilities, gardening, trash hauling, and everything else—then Bob owes the IRS income tax on just $500. Indeed, with smart use of depreciation and other breaks, a landlord like Bob can end up pocketing that money and live his life virtually income-tax free.

Operating expenses for Bill, the home owner, equal the same $2,000 a month. But Bill is allowed to reduce his taxes by choosing to claim either a standard deduction ($10,900 for married couples in 2008) or a deduction for paying mortgage interest (about $12,500 for a median-priced home bought in 2008 with a 90% mortgage loan).

Because Bill could take the standard deduction whether he owned his home or not, the actual value of the mortgage-interest deduction should be figured on only the difference between his total interest payment and the standard deduction—$1,600. Because Bill is in the 25% tax bracket, the real value of the home-buyer's tax break? A measly $400. (Yes, there are other deductions available to tax itemizers, but we're looking here at just the biggest—the mortgage-interest deduction.)

And that small benefit will disappear for Bill in just a couple of years, as the standard deduction adjusts upward and the interest portion of his monthly mortgage payments declines.

Q: So, should you always buy more house? The more you spend, the more the government pays you.

A: That's like saying, "I'll spend a dollar to get 25 cents back." You're still out 75 cents.

It's true that the mortgage deduction becomes more valuable the more expensive the house and the higher your tax bracket. It can mean all the difference in the world to home buyers in high-cost areas like California or New York. But even those buyers should never spend money on something that costs hundreds of thousands of dollars and takes three decades to pay for just because there's a tax deduction.

If Mike, Bill's 35%-tax-bracket boss, takes out a $2 million mortgage on a waterfront villa, his mortgage interest would come to more than $121,000 the first year. That translates into a $42,000 mortgage-interest deduction—much better than the standard deduction of $10,900. Still nothing to get excited over. Mike could pay cash for the house, not take a tax deduction at all and still come out way ahead.

Even with the deduction, Mike is paying $80,000 rent (interest) on the borrowed money—money that neither buys his house nor comes back in the tax subsidy. It just goes down the same black hole that sucks up any other renter's money.

Q: I have to live somewhere! I have to pay something for a place to live!

A. Yes, you do. But don't confuse your real "I-have-to-pay-something" costs with the cost of renting borrowed money. The "I-have-to-pay-something" costs are the actual expenses of living in your own home—property taxes, maintenance, insurance, repairs—costs that anyone owning a property would have.

If Mike paid cash for his $2 million place, he'd still have to pay property taxes, painters, plumbers, electricians and all the other "I-have-to-pay-something" costs.

Q: Wouldn't I be paying those same costs if I rented? Landlords pass along their operating costs to their tenants.

A: Yes, successful landlords have mastered the art of using other people's money to pay for their buildings, including charging tenants for upkeep and improvements. But no, individual renters don't pay all their landlord's expenses.

If you live in a multiple-unit building, repair and maintenance costs are spread among all the tenants. Even if you rent a single-family home, though, you aren't going to pay all the freight.

Suppose you rent a house for $2,000 a month, and the septic system fails. The landlord is obligated to repair it or replace it as soon as possible. The landlord may even be required to pay for you to live somewhere else while the septic system is inoperable.

The landlord could be on the hook immediately for $20,000 or more, but he can't demand payment from you or suddenly raise your rent to cover those costs. After the current lease is up, the landlord will almost certainly raise the rent, but not enough to recover all his costs quickly. Maybe he'll raise the rent to $2,500—a substantial increase, to be sure, but not enough to recover the cost of the septic system right away.

The typical home owner is in a similar boat as the landlord—but with no renter to help with the bills. When the septic tank goes, just tack on another twenty grand to the cost of owning a home.

Q: Yes, but home owner's costs are much more manageable. They don't go up every year like rents.

A: *One* monthly cost doesn't go up. Yes, if you have a fixed-rate mortgage, your monthly mortgage payment will remain fixed for the life of the loan. But every other home-owing cost goes up and up as relentlessly as a landlord raises rents. Ask Florida's home owners about their insurance rates after hurricanes blew through the state. Skyrocketing oil prices have sent Frost Belt heating bills through the roof while deregulated electricity rates have forced Sun Belters to turn off their air conditioners.

And rising real-estate taxes have sparked Proposition 13–style taxpayer revolts from Arizona to Maine.

Q: How much does a house really cost?

A: You can easily end up spending three times the purchase price of a house. Today's buyer of a typical $300,000 single-family home who takes out a thirty-year loan will end up paying more than the price of the house just in interest. Add thirty years of property taxes, insurance, regular maintenance and a couple of big-ticket repairs (like a new septic system) or improvements (like a new kitchen and a new master suite), and the lifetime cost of buying the home could easily top out at more than $1 million.

THE COSTS OF BUYING A HOME OVER THIRTY YEARS		2007
Purchase price		$290,000
Down payment		$58,000
Mortgage principal		$232,000
Interest @ 6.41% (before tax)		$291,000
Taxes and insurance	($6,000/year)	$180,000
Maintenance	($300/month)	$108,000
Major repairs and improvements		$300,000
Total costs		**$1,169,000**

Q: Yes, but the house will be worth much, much more.

A: Maybe, maybe not. Whether you come out ahead really depends on where and when you buy. Even cash buyers might be surprised to see that they can't be assured of always making a profit.

If you had bought a house in Los Angeles in 1990, just as the Cold War ended, local defense industries shut down and the local real-estate market turned downward, you would have had to wait a decade for your home's value to return to what you paid. If you bought in Dallas in 1986, as the oil boom went bust, your home wouldn't have appreciated at all before 1998. People who bought houses in the hottest bubble markets— roughly from 2000 to 2006—may not see any price appreciation before 2015 or so. Some economists believe prices won't recover their bubble-era highs (adjusted for inflation) for fifteen to twenty years.

Here's a simplified rundown on a typical single-family home—a house bought for $50,000 in 1977. Numbers are based on national appreciation rates as reported by the Office of Federal Housing Enterprise Oversight (OFHEO); modest estimates of other home-owning costs are included (not adjusted for inflation). The chart compares the costs of buying a house

BORROWING VERSUS PAYING CASH (1977-2007)		Mortgage	Cash
1977 purchase price		$50,000	$50,000
2007 sale price		**$288,000**	**$288,000**
Down payment		$10,000	$0
Mortgage principal		$40,000	$0
Interest @ 8.72% (before tax)		$74,000	$0
Taxes and insurance	($3,000/year)	$90,000	$90,000
Maintenance	($150/month)	$54,000	$54,000
Major repairs and improvements		$150,000	$150,000
Real-estate commission and other sale costs		$23,000	$23,000
Total costs		**$441,000**	**$317,000**
Profit/(loss)		**($153,000)**	**($29,000)**

Note: 8.72% was the average mortgage interest rate in 1977; the 2007 price is based on OFHEO calculations.

with a long-term mortgage versus paying cash for the same house. Both scenarios have "I-have-to-pay-something" costs, but the borrower is hit with the additional pain of interest costs. (To keep things simple, there are limited transaction costs, no additional borrowing to finance improvements and no refinancing costs, all of which would drive the expenses even higher.) You'll see, it's really not a pretty picture for either buyer.

Q: THOSE NUMBERS DON'T SEEM REALISTIC FOR WHERE I LIVE. YOU CAN'T BUY A HOUSE HERE FOR THAT KIND OF MONEY.

A: To be sure, not everyone did so badly as the national average. OFHEO's Home Price Index calculator puts the average 1977–2007 appreciation for a house in the ever-pricey San Francisco metropolitan area at 1,133%, compared with the national average of just 475% *(http://www.ofheo.gov/)*. So if you bought that $50,000 house in San Francisco in 1977, it would be worth about $617,000 today, and, assuming much the same costs of ownership, you'd make a true profit of $223,000. You would have done well in other coastal metro regions, too. The comparable house would be worth about $591,000 in Los Angeles (up 1,082%), $545,000 in New York (990%) and $430,000 in Washington (760%).

Some other big cities didn't fare as well. You'd be in the red in Chicago, where home values rose 458% and the house would be worth $279,000. Your house would be valued at only about $175,000 (250%) in Dallas and just $144,000 in Houston (189%).

Q: EVEN IF I HAD BOUGHT IN TEXAS, I'D STILL BE LIVING "RENT FREE" FOR THIRTY YEARS. LOOK AT ALL THE MONEY I'VE SAVED OVER THE YEARS BY NOT PAYING RENT.

A: Living "rent free" is moving in with your parents or your wealthy lover. You didn't live rent free. At best, you had some

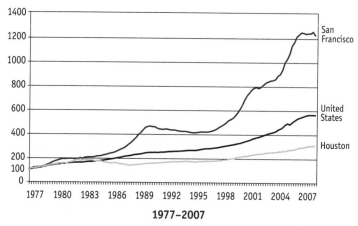

THIRTY YEARS OF HOME PRICE INCREASES

1977–2007

Source: OFHEO.

of your rent money subsidized by the government and then some more rebated when you sold your property.

Home buyers like to argue that the "imputed rent"—the money that they didn't spend on rent—should be counted somehow as part of their housing profits.

That's false logic. Economists invented "imputed rent" to compensate for a macroeconomic anomaly: as home owner-ship increases, the amount of national income contributed by rents paid to landlords decreases, but the activity of occupying and living in properties continues as before. So, the econo-mists invented imputed rent—what they describe as rent that a home owner pays to himself in lieu of what he would have paid to a landlord—as a way of accounting for the apparent lost economic activity. But like particle physics or string theory, im-puted rent has nothing to do with the world we actually live in, nor does it contribute to home owners' returns on their in-vestments.

As they say in *Jerry Maguire*, "Show me the money!" If you're a home owner, imputed rent doesn't put one extra dol-lar in your pocket. It has no impact at all on your day-to-day finances. And there's no way to account for imputed rent on an income statement. Indeed, on a personal-finance level, imputed rent doesn't exist; it's only money not spent. (As if you could mitigate the adverse effects of going into debt to buy an $80,000 Mercedes by imputing all the taxi and bus fares you "save.")

On the nation's profit-and-loss statement, imputed rent makes a difference. But any way you look at your personal ledger, you only substituted a monthly mortgage payment for a monthly rent payment.

Q: WHEN I SELL, THOUGH, I GET THE MONEY I'VE SPENT BACK, RIGHT? THAT'S THE REAL PLUS OF BUYING. ALL THOSE MORTGAGE PAYMENTS AND MORE ARE PUT BACK IN MY POCKET WHEN I SELL.

A: That's assuming that everything breaks your way. Remember, if you add up all your home-owning costs over the years, the odds are that you have spent more than your apparent profit when you sell.

Yes, hold on to your house long enough, and you're certain to get something back, your rebate. But if you stretched yourself to buy a bigger, more expensive house, then you almost certainly lost more lucrative investing opportunities along the way while you were spending your money buying the house.

If you don't sell at the top of the market, you could see stagnant or falling values for a while. There have been real-estate bubbles before. San Francisco values peaked in early 1990 before falling for the next eight years, and Houston has seen only grindingly slow appreciation for two decades.

Q: ANYTHING'S BETTER THAN NOTHING AT
ALL, RIGHT? EVEN IF I LIVED IN HOUSTON AND
DIDN'T SEE GREAT PRICE RUN-UPS, THE
INCREASE IN VALUE IS STILL MONEY THAT I
WOULDN'T SEE OTHERWISE. EVEN GETTING
JUST SOME OF MY MONEY BACK IS BETTER THAN
GETTING NONE.

A: There's another kick in the pants. You haven't gotten any
money back yet. All you have right now is a house that's thirty
years older than when you moved into it. Houses aren't liquid
like real savings accounts. You can't just insert your ATM card
and take out some cash. A house is not even like a stock portfolio; you can't go online and click the "sell" button and have
your money automatically deposited in your account a couple
of days later.

One of the unfortunate symptoms of the bubble was the
constant fixation with climbing home values. People watched
their home values like 1990s tech-stock traders. As house values
rose, home owners felt wealthier month by month, often borrowing money to spend on things they probably didn't need.

That's unfortunate because the home-owning experience
isn't at all comparable to stock investing. In order to realize
your home owner's windfall, you have to borrow against your
house or you have to sell it. If you borrow with a "cash-out" refinance loan, then you have, in effect, just taken your house to
a pawnshop. You will need to pay that new loan back, with interest, before you will actually own your house.

If you sell your house, what are you going to do with that
big check in your pocket after you've walked around for a couple of hours feeling richer than you've ever been? You'll probably spend most of it buying another house.

Q: YES, BUT WHATEVER PROFIT I DO MAKE, WILL BE CAPITAL-GAINS TAX FREE!

A: That break is more illusion than substance. It does indeed give the sellers of expensive properties a nice break, but it means relatively little to people living in average homes.

Under current law, a married couple selling a house isn't required to pay taxes on the first $500,000 of profit ($250,000 for singles). It sounds great. And it's one of the most touted attractions of home owning.

But borrow money to buy a moderately priced home, like most of us do, and the capital-gains tax advantage withers. You still get the difference between the price you paid and the price you sold, but it's going to be way, way less than $500,000. The real bear comes in, though, because unlike any other investment, you aren't allowed to deduct any of your holding costs (your "I-have-to-pay-something" costs) from the gross sales price.

Yes, you can deduct the costs of actually selling, but that's it. None of the actual costs of owning and operating the property are subtracted from the sale price. And that, as you've already seen, can exceed the total sales price.

Other investments aren't treated that way. A professional stock trader can sell one hundred shares of stock online, and deduct from his gross profit not only the broker's commission and the annual account fee, but also the cost of his computer, his *Wall Street Journal* subscription, the Internet connection, even some of his electric bill. If he borrowed the money to buy the stock, he can write off all the interest. Then, if he still has a gain, he can offset that with a loss from selling another stock.

Landlords have a similar deal—writing off dollar for dollar all of the owning and operating costs that home owners just pay and pay and pay.

Can you, the home owner, write off having your house painted ten years ago? Nope. Repair the roof in 2004? Sorry.

Home owner's association fees? No way. Property taxes? Not if you pay the alternative minimum tax. Replace the rotted piling under the porch? Fuhgeddaboudit.

And the ultimate insult: if you lose money on your house because the market has soured and maybe you have to sell immediately because you lose your job—you can't write off your loss.

What's the big capital-gains break for most home owners? No tax on a profit that is probably not a real profit at all. And no write off for a devastating loss that will affect you for years.

Q: I'LL DOWNSIZE, FIND A SMALLER, CHEAPER HOUSE, BUY IT AND THEN INVEST THE REST OF THE MONEY.

A: Home prices tend to rise or fall across an entire market. If you want to stay in the same metropolitan region and save a big chunk of your rebated nest egg, you should be prepared to go significantly downscale, probably more than you'd prefer. You will most likely have to move to a much, much smaller place or to a much less desirable neighborhood.

Let's look at a complete, thirty-year rundown on a house in the pricey Washington metropolitan area.

This table shows the costs of buying and owning a hypothetical home in suburban Washington. The house was bought in 1977 for $55,000 and sold in 2007 for $860,000. At the sale closing, the sellers pocketed about $550,000, an apparent 10,900% return on their $5,000 down payment. But further examination of their costs—typical for a house owned for three decades—makes clear that the sellers made a nice but far more modest profit of just $175,000. Sellers elsewhere could easily end up losing money. (For the record, if you perform a proper analysis, computing the owner's "internal rate of return" over the years, the house makes an annual 3.83%—or .83% after inflation.)

NOT AS RICH AS YOU THINK

Year	Home value	Loan to value	Annual payments	Principal	Mortgage balance	Transaction costs
1977	$55,000	90%	$4,707.36	$361.59	$49,638	$1,500
1978	$62,650	79%	$4,707.36	$394.41	$49,244	
1979	$72,671	67%	$4,707.36	$430.21	$48,814	
1980	$80,170	60%	$4,707.36	$469.26	$48,345	
1981	$86,784	55%	$4,707.36	$511.86	$47,833	
1982	$89,824	53%	$4,707.36	$558.32	$47,274	
1983	$101,074	60%	$7,420.44	$1,381.86	$60,892	$800
1984	$105,088	56%	$7,420.44	$1,545.91	$59,347	
1985	$113,135	51%	$7,420.44	$1,730.26	$57,616	
1986	$119,838	50%	$6,419.88	$320.57	$59,679	$2,000
1987	$133,593	44%	$6,419.88	$354.80	$59,325	
1988	$155,653	38%	$6,419.88	$392.71	$58,932	
1989	$176,111	33%	$6,419.88	$434.65	$58,497	
1990	$187,270	31%	$6,419.88	$481.07	$58,016	
1991	$186,441	31%	$6,419.88	$532.44	$57,484	
1992	$189,534	30%	$6,419.88	$589.30	$56,894	
1993	$189,166	30%	$6,419.88	$652.24	$56,242	
1994	$191,136	29%	$6,419.88	$721.89	$55,520	
1995	$184,139	30%	$6,419.88	$798.99	$54,721	
1996	$326,639	58%	$16,428.84	$1,648.01	$188,352	$4,000
1997	$320,896	58%	$16,428.84	$1,781.42	$186,571	
1998	$329,916	56%	$16,428.84	$1,925.64	$184,645	
1999	$339,592	54%	$16,428.84	$2,081.53	$182,563	
2000	$360,036	50%	$16,428.84	$2,250.05	$180,313	
2001	$401,986	44%	$16,428.84	$2,432.20	$177,881	
2002	$447,556	39%	$16,428.84	$2,629.12	$175,252	
2003	$496,404	35%	$16,428.84	$2,841.95	$172,410	
2004	$566,101	44%	$17,679.12	$3,162.89	$246,837	$2,500
2005	$703,124	35%	$17,679.12	$3,352.65	$243,484	
2006	$860,217	28%	$17,679.12	$3,553.76	$239,931	
SUBTOTALS				$40,321.56		$10,800
AFTER-TAX (33% bracket)						$7,236
SELL:	**$860,000**				**($239,931)**	**($58,836)**

Note: Home value is based on the OFHEO Home Price Index for Washington area (1Q'77–3Q'06); values were readjusted in '83 and '96 to reflect improvements; interest rates and points are averages at the time as reported by Freddie Mac; property taxes are estimates at 2% of that year's value; insurance estimates at .5% of value.

Interest paid	Property taxes	Insurance	Repairs and maintenance	Major events over period of ownership
$4,346	$1,100	$275	$360	Purchase: $55,000; $5,000 down; 8.72%, 30-years, 1.1points.
$4,313	$1,253	$313	$371	
$4,277	$1,453	$363	$382	
$4,238	$1,603	$401	$393	European vacation
$4,196	$1,736	$434	$405	First baby
$4,149	$1,796	$449	$417	
$6,039	$2,021	$505	$430	Kitchen remodel, second mortgage $15,000; 13.24%, 10 years, 2.1 points
$5,875	$2,102	$525	$443	Second baby
$5,690	$2,263	$566	$456	Third baby
$6,099	$2,397	$599	$470	Refinance: $60,000; 10.19%, 30 years, 2.2 points
$6,065	$2,672	$668	$10,484	Exterior painting: $10000
$6,027	$3,113	$778	$499	
$5,985	$3,522	$881	$513	
$5,939	$3,745	$936	$529	
$5,887	$3,729	$932	$545	
$5,831	$3,791	$948	$561	Disney World vacation
$5,768	$3,783	$946	$578	
$5,698	$3,823	$956	$595	
$5,621	$3,683	$921	$613	
$14,781	$6,533	$1,633	$632	Major renovation, refinance: $190,000; 7.81%, 30 years, 1.7 points
$14,647	$6,418	$1,604	$650	
$14,503	$6,598	$1,650	$670	First child starts college
$14,347	$6,792	$1,698	$25,690	New roof: $25,000
$14,179	$7,201	$1,800	$711	
$13,997	$8,040	$2,010	$732	Second child starts college
$13,800	$8,951	$2,238	$754	Third child starts college
$13,587	$9,928	$2,482	$777	
$14,516	$11,322	$2,831	$800	Refinance: $250,000; 5.84%, 30 years, 0.7 points ($75,000 cash out)
$14,326	$14,062	$3,516	$20,824	Renovate patio/lawn: $20,000
$14,125	$17,204	$4,301	$849	Last child finishes college
$258,851	$152,635	$38,159	$72,132	
$173,430	$102,265	$38,159	$72,132	
($173,430)	($102,265)	($38,159)	($72,132)	$175,247

As you can see, these home owners have done rather well. Their modest $55,000 home is now worth a whopping $860,000. If they sell, they will walk out the door with a tax-free check for about $550,000. But they're facing an expensive market where the median price of a condo is two-thirds the cost of a single-family home. They don't have enough money to make the most obvious move down—from their house to a comparable mortgage-free condo that would cost them something in the neighborhood of $575,000.

Q: I'LL MOVE TO SOMEPLACE CHEAPER.

A: You still face borrowing or spending all or most of your cash on your new house—and you will still have maintenance, property taxes, insurance and other "I-have-to-pay-something" costs.

If our Washington couple chooses to leave and move to a cheaper housing market, they will still have costs greater than they think. Popular retirement communities are usually cheaper than big metropolitan areas, but they are not so cheap that sale proceeds will plant them on a country club fairway and pay for the lifestyle that goes with it.

According to Coldwell Banker's often-cited home-comparison calculator, a house comparable to the place in Washington would cost $439,000 in Fort Myers, Florida, or $407,000 in Orlando. The couple would do a little better moving to Tucson, Arizona, where the comparable house costs $281,000—leaving the Washington home sellers less than half of their rebate windfall.

So yes, cashing out of a pricey market on one of the coasts could give them enough money to buy a nice place on a golf course somewhere in the Sun Belt. And if they're lucky they might have $200,000 or $300,000 left over. That will generate just $10,000 to $15,000 a year of income, hardly a ticket to the good life.

Q: WHY SHOULD I BUY A HOUSE? YOU MAKE
IT SOUND LIKE THERE'S NO GOOD FINANCIAL
REASON TO BUY, BUT EVERYONE I KNOW HAS
A HOUSE OR WANTS ONE.

A: Owning a home is a wonderful thing. And smart home owning—approaching home ownership with realism and financial
prudence—can pay off well. Anything to reduce your borrowing expenses and remodeling costs will provide a handsome
return.

On a broader level, home owning is fundamental to a nation built by wave after wave of economic and social strivers.
Family-owned homes provide solid foundations for later generations to build on the material accomplishments of their an-
cestors. It isn't necessary to even pass along significant wealth,
just the point of view that develops from property ownership
and the discipline it takes to achieve it. Indeed, if you want to
gauge someone's potential to achieve financial well-being in
his or her lifetime, here's the first question you should ask:
"Did your grandparents own their home?"

A house may not be the investment most home owners
think it is, but buying a home can be a good, sound way to
spend money and build a future.

And beyond the dollars and cents, the main reasons most
people buy homes—for shelter, security, a sense of ownership,
community and to raise families—have little to do with personal finances and lots to do with a sense of personal worth
and self-esteem.

Those are not things easily quantified, but they shouldn't
be ignored either.

Q: What can I do if I've planned too much of my financial life around my investment in my home?

A: That's what we will explore in the coming chapters. If you're a first-time buyer, you can use many of the lessons here to approach home buying with a more realistic, more financially savvy attitude. If you are retired or approaching retirement and want to tap your home's equity, you can learn to maximize your return without seriously downgrading your lifestyle.

And if you're somewhere in between, living in your home and wondering how you can better manage it, you can still rein in your expenses and diversify your investments. Wherever you may be, you can use the lessons of this book to reconsider the conventional wisdom about buying a house.

Do the math. Don't buy or hold on to a house that's too big for your needs or so expensive that you must strain to pay for it simply because "it's a good investment."

It's not.

CHAPTER 2

HOME OWNING IN A TROUBLED MARKET

When every piece of furniture and your underwear are taken by the bank, when you lose your house in Florida, in New York, in Amsterdam and L.A., when your wife is dying and your son abandons you, you don't feel very good.

—AL GOLDSTEIN

Imagine that someone's slapped a big sign on the United States: 25% off!

When prices fall at Target or Macy's, you and your neighbors may rush over to the mall to pick up some bargains. When Toyota and Honda mark down their current inventory to make way for new models, hordes of buyers will storm the nation's auto strips come Saturday. When prices fall on Wall Street, every stock transaction involves a buyer expecting prices to go back up soon enough.

So, why when prices fall on Nightingale Lane or Shady Oaks Drive does the whole country get depressed?

As we have seen since the mortgage meltdown began in 2007, the home-buying-owning-selling economy is so vital to the nation's well-being that people everywhere feel a lot less wealthy and a lot less willing to spend. Home prices fall, and credit dries up. Bankers panic. Business managers cancel multibillion-dollar merger deals. Real-estate agents and local builders pore over the help wanted ads, and local politicians tighten their budgets.

The home-owning economy grinds slower and slower. Sellers take houses off the market and cancel their own plans to move to new homes. Meanwhile, home shoppers grow cautious, thinking they shouldn't buy if prices are going to fall further in the future.

Broadly declining home prices hardly signal the collapse of the nation's economy, but they do indicate the end of the home-owning world as we have known it for the past sixty years.

For the foreseeable future, house prices are likely to remain stagnant at best and, in many previously hot markets, to continue declining. At the Chicago Mercantile Exchange, professional traders bet on the trends in home values in a house-price futures market. The betting there is that house values in ten of the nation's largest markets are unlikely to bottom out for a long, long time. Indeed, in the fall of 2007, when prices were already depressed, traders were predicting an average decline of 23% by November 2011, betting that Miami prices will fall by 29% and those in San Francisco by 26%. Even in Chicago, long the most steady gainer—and the major metropolitan area that historically most closely reflects the national trend—traders were betting on a 10% decline.

Moreover, the real-estate bubble disrupted the balance between income levels and home values, and things might have to get even worse before they get better. Brett Arends of the *Wall Street Journal Online* calculated that house prices in California, Arizona and Florida would need to fall 30% to 40% *from depressed 2008 levels* just to settle back into the historic equilibrium between home prices and personal incomes. If prices just stagnate, it will take a decade for incomes to catch up.

There's no guarantee, of course, that the pessimists at the Chicago Merc or elsewhere are right. Although prices are still falling, it's possible they could bottom out in 2009 or 2010. But there's also no guarantee that they won't bottom out until 2012, or later.

What is clear, however, is that many home owners are facing broad stock-market-style home-value declines of a magnitude quite unlike any the United States has seen since the 1930s.

While these declines might put a dent in a current home owner's net worth, remember that you lose money only when you sell. If you have been in your home for a long time and plan to stay in it, you will probably weather the downturn and do all right because eventually there will be a market bottom and, beyond that, prices will start going up again. Eventually.

Still, as in any downturn in any other market—stocks, oil, gold, even tulips—there will be winners and losers. Here's a quick rundown of how buyers stack up:

- **First-time home buyers.** This could turn out to be the greatest "buyer's market" in U.S. history. Smart, cool-headed house shopping could well land you in your dream home at half or less of what you might have spent five years ago.

- **Early-cycle home buyers.** It could be rough. If you bought your first house within the last ten years, the good news is that, like first-time buyers, you face a new, much more affordable move-up market. But the bad news is that your home value could fall so much that you will lose most of your modest equity and, in a severe downturn, you could wind up "upside down" with a mortgage balance that is much greater than the market value of the house.

- **Mid-cycle home buyers.** If you entered the housing market in the late 1980s or early '90s, even if you have moved up since your first home, you probably have sufficient equity in your house to weather all but a doomsday decline. You have already passed through one down-and-up cycle. So if you feel you really want to move up to a nicer house and want to take advantage of the downturn, you will have to scale back your expectations on the price you will get for your home. On the plus side, the home you want to buy will be cheaper, too. My advice, however: don't move unless you have the cash to buy without selling your home.

- **Late-cycle home buyers.** If you entered the housing market before the *first* Bush administration, you are probably within sight of paying off your mortgage (at last!) and are eyeing new uses for your monthly mortgage check. Again, even if you have moved up once or twice and are still several years from paying off the mortgage loan, you probably have sufficient equity to weather this down market. Finish paying off your loan and try to save more for your retirement in ten to fifteen years.

- **Home owners.** If you are still working and are no longer buying your house, you're probably now in a position to stash away cash at a prodigious rate. That's good. You'll need it. You won't be able to count on selling your house for the kind of money that you had hoped would fund your retirement. If you are already retired, you will have to rethink any plans you had about selling or borrowing against your home equity as part of your retirement savings.

WHY HOMES VALUES ARE FALLING

First things first: Home prices are not going down everywhere. Real-estate markets are local, extremely local. Prices may hold relatively stable in the best close-in neighborhoods but fall 40% in the distant suburbs. Even during the bubble era, some areas saw much more modest prices and price increases than others. Attractive Sun Belt cities such as Atlanta and Nashville didn't experience the huge price run-ups and haven't, so far, experienced huge falloffs. As late as the spring of 2008, in Charlotte, North Carolina, prices were still rising.

Through the first half of the decade, home buyers in Buffalo could purchase good single-family homes in good neighborhoods for what Los Angeles buyers were making as down payments. In some of the Great Plains states, local officials tried to stem the century-long exodus of young people by, literally, giving away homes. Canadian Internet phenomenon Kyle MacDonald started with a red paperclip and spent 2005 and 2006 swapping up for even more valuable items until he traded the town leaders of Kipling, Saskatchewan, a one-line movie role for an empty three-bedroom, 1,100-square-foot house.

Meanwhile, buyers in Florida, Nevada or Arizona fought to bid homes up thousands of dollars over asking prices. And houses in metropolitan areas rose in value far more than in rural areas. Even the outer boroughs of New York City saw population increases and surges in home values as the tired hamlets and cities of upstate New York sank even further into their decades-long depressions.

If you are reading this book, the odds are that the prices in your town are on the downward trend. That's because home values are generally on the downside of a cycle that peaked after the stock market collapse in 2000 and the September 11, 2001, terrorist attacks. Those events ushered in a short period of historically low interest rates that made buying a home remarkably affordable.

Let's put it in perspective: In May 2000, just after the Nasdaq reached its Internet bubble peak, a $200,000 thirty-year mortgage carried a fixed 8.54% interest rate—costing a home buyer about $1,543 a month. Three years later, in June 2003, the interest rate had fallen to 5.23%, and a home buyer could afford a $280,000 mortgage for the same monthly payment. Home builders and home sellers were more than happy to help out with higher prices.

Lenders helped, too. They came up with all sorts of new financing schemes—from zero-down "option ARMs" that let borrowers decide just how much they wanted to pay each month to interest-only loans to forty-year mortgages. As interest rates fell and prices rose, adjustable-rate mortgages—the time bombs that exploded in the sub-prime mortgage crisis of 2007— became an even better deal. One-year ARMs in July 2000 carried a 7.29% interest rate, but the rate was just 3.52% in June 2003. The buyer who could afford only a $200,000 mortgage in 2000 could now afford a $345,000 adjustable-rate mortgage— and often without having to make a down payment.

No wonder prices skyrocketed, and houses were all of a sudden worth a lot more.

According to the Census Bureau, the national median home price rose from $169,000 in 2000 to $246,000 in 2006. On the coasts the jumps were even greater: in the Northeast the median price peaked at $346,000 and $406,000 in the West.

House prices got seriously out of whack. The traditional benchmark for prices—the ratio of rents to property prices— hit historic lows. The very modest income increases seen by the vast majority of Americans were rapidly outstripped by escalating prices, even as the stock market and the economy recovered. By 2004, nearly one in three American households were spending one-third of their incomes on housing, reported Harvard's Joint Center for Housing Studies. One in eight was spending more than 50%.

Grossly irresponsible lending practices fed the mania and pumped up the bubble. And it wasn't the illegal lending that was the scandal; it was what was legal—"no doc" deals that didn't even require borrowers to have jobs, or Internet applications where, like in the *New Yorker* cartoon, no one knew the online borrowers were dogs. All in all, it was a not-so-wonderful banking life where Old Man Potter had put crazy Uncle Billy in charge of the lending department.

On top of everything, home buyers were thinking like renters, looking only at what they had to spend each month to move into a new house. They convinced themselves that they were investing, too, of course, as they saw house prices rising and rising. Like dotcom stocks in 1999, home prices were just going up and up. A home buyer with nothing down and no more financial interest in his home than his monthly interest-only payment could see his net worth shoot up as the leveraged value of his new house went up 10%, 20%, 30% in just a year or two.

A house "bought" in 2004 for $300,000 was "worth" $432,000 two years later, a $132,000 gain for the "owner."

Sound familiar? It was practically a bedrooms-and-baths replay of the highly leveraged stock-buying frenzy of the late 1920s, when the proverbial shoe-shine boy borrowed 100% of the price of a stock and then became a paper millionaire as more shoe-shine boys with more borrowed money bid up stock prices higher and higher. Until they stopped.

Like latecomers to the stock-market frenzy, first-time home buyers in the bubble era believed they had to get into the housing market or they would be left forever at the mercy of their landlords. Besides, their thinking went, buying a house is the best two-fer deal: "It's a savings account that you can live in for just a bit more every month than you were already paying in rent." So, they swapped writing rent checks for mortgage checks.

Move-up buyers sold and doubled down. They had little real equity because they had not paid off much of the mortgages on their first properties, but they had the inflated equity of bubble-market appreciation, which they used to buy more expensive houses—again paying just a bit more each month.

Meanwhile, the home-buying cabal pressed on with its "real-estate-can't-fail" pitch that promised ever-greater returns for home buyers.

It was, by any definition, a financial pyramid. Just like the stockbrokers giving shoe-shiners margin loans, lackadaisical mortgage lenders shoveled hundreds of thousands of dollars

Type of home	Overall	What's good?
Single-family detached house	Long the gold standard of home owning; abundant supply in older and brand-new neighborhoods; wide variety of styles, sizes, lots	Own land as well as building; can alter exterior changes and expansion as local laws allow; privacy
Town house (planned unit development, row house)	Common in older, inner-city areas and, increasingly, in suburbs where local government policies and land prices make more traditional single-family projects prohibitively expensive for developers to build	Cheaper than single-family detached home; units usually include small outdoor space; large enough for families; more privacy than condo apartment; in older areas ownership includes land; newer town home developments feature community amenities such as pools, tennis courts, etc.
Multi-family (two, three or four-unit buildings)	Common in older, inner-city areas but largely absent from suburbs; recently some communities have allowed new "in-law" units and small apartments attached to single-family homes	Owner-occupier can use rents from tenants to cover home-owning expenses; own land; can alter and expand as local regulations allow; opportunities to increase revenues
Condominium	Long popular in suburbs as well as in cities; major building boom in inner cities during the last decade or so; ownership of individual units with home owner's association owning common areas	Units in top-line buildings can command per-square-foot prices greater than comparable single-family homes; staff for maintenance and repairs; community amenities; most developments better suited for singles, empty nesters than families with children
Cooperative apartment (co-op)	Small niche in housing market; extremely rare outside New York, Washington, Chicago and a few other big cities; no individual ownership; owners occupy units because they hold shares in nonprofit corporation that owns the building	Exclusivity; highly selective process for acquiring units; staff for maintenance and repairs; community amenities; most developments better suited for singles, empty nesters than families with children

JUST A HOUSE

What's bad?	Financial outlook
Owner is responsible for all repairs and maintenance; high energy use; auto-dependent neighborhoods	Prices relatively stable in established, upscale neighborhoods; expect declines in marginal areas, newest developments
Usual drawbacks of close living—lack of privacy, common walls, noise, etc.; alterations may be difficult without approvals from neighbors; houses in older neighborhoods may not have garages or parking spaces	Older homes in upscale neighborhoods likely to continue commanding high prices; houses in gentrifying neighborhoods also likely to maintain values; outlook less positive for developments in outlying areas
Landlording, property management required; tenant issues older; buildings need frequent maintenance; lack of privacy	Mixed; short-term prospects are good as some former home owners revert to renting and younger (Generation Y) renters on increase; long-term chances for appreciation and rent increase less certain as renters will be able to buy more, cheaper homes
Apartment living by another name—lack of privacy, common walls, noise, etc.; alterations may be difficult; lack of facilities for children	Traditionally low appreciation outside best buildings in biggest cities; city condo values outperformed co-ops in bubble era but are likely to fall back in the aftermath; values in outlying areas uncertain
Units in top buildings can be very expensive; no or limited mortgages allowed; building restrictions on alterations, activities; not family friendly; prices lagged behind condos in bubble era	Stringent ownership and financial-responsibility requirements are likely to shield co-ops from foreclosure problems; prices sensitive to general downturn; competition from cheaper condominiums

to buyers who lacked the incomes and the financial sophistication to keep their homes.

Even well-to-do home buyers were sucked in. Although the concentration of questionable loans was higher in poorer communities, the number of sub-prime mortgages carrying high reset rates and onerously higher payments also rose sharply in middle-class and wealthier communities. A *Wall Street Journal* analysis found that one-fourth of the 43.6 million home loans made between 2004 and 2006 fell into this category. As home prices accelerated, even affluent families turned to sub-prime loans to buy expensive homes they could not have qualified for under conventional lending standards.

"We had an aggressive home-mortgage industry trying to get people into homes they couldn't afford at a time when home prices were very high. It turned out to be a house of cards," Karl Case, an economics professor at Wellesley College, told my *Wall Street Journal* colleagues Rick Brooks and Constance Mitchell Ford.

The government moved aggressively in 2008 to deal with the crisis. New laws made it easier for home owners to avoid foreclosure, lending limits were lifted, and there was even a new tax credit for first-time buyers.

Still, there were more than 2 million homes in foreclosure by 2008, with more expected through 2009 and 2010. New, tighter credit requirements for even well-qualified buyers. Multibillion-dollar losses for lenders and Wall Street investment houses. Thousands of layoffs in the financial, real-estate and real-estate-dependent industries. And millions of home owners, including Baby Boomers quickly approaching their retirements, dumbstruck as they watch the value of their biggest assets decline month after month, year after year.

What's the downside? A decade or more of falling or stagnant prices in much of the country. If the traders on the Chicago Merc are right, the median house price in the United States in 2011 will be about where it was in 2001, wiping out much of the housing boom's value increases with no guaran-

IT'S ALL ABOUT LEVERAGE

Leverage is a powerful financial concept that is absolutely vital to the free operation of business, but its benefits to home buyers are grossly oversold.

It's simple. You pay a little, borrow a lot and end up with all the ownership. That works great if you are making software and need a bank loan to get your product to market. If you are borrowing just to buy a bigger car or a bigger house, though, you are deceiving yourself.

The home-buying industry's most basic argument for houses as investments is based on some variation of the value of leverage. A typical pitch: "You can buy a $300,000 house with just $15,000 down. If the house value goes up just 5%, you'll double your money!"

From a financial point of view, that argument has problems, not the least of which is if you are making mortgage payments, then you lose much of the advantage of the price appreciation.

For decades, the traditional standard was to put down 20% on a house and obtain a bank loan for 80%. But the old standards went by the wayside. First came 10% down loans, then 5%—or less. Early in the decade, buyers were encouraged to take out 100% loans. And even with today's more stringent post-bubble lending standards, it's possible to buy fixer-upper properties with no money down and mortgage-rehab loans covering 125% of the property's price.

Leverage works best and the investment is safest when the payback period is relatively short and the borrower makes a substantial down payment.

Sophisticated borrowers and lenders operate within a system that encourages leveraged transactions but puts strong limits on them to discourage recklessness. When an investor buys a stock on margin, he or she typically puts down 50% cash and borrows 50% from a stockbroker. The buyer of an office building or large apartment houses may have to put down 25% to 35% of the purchase price and borrow the rest. The thinking: the more of his own money that an entrepreneur has tied up in a deal—the more "skin he has in the game," it's called—the safer the loan and the greater the likelihood that the purchased enterprise will be profitable.

How does leverage work for the rest of us? At least up until the credit crunch of 2007, it was more or less anything goes. The lending safeguards imposed on sophisticated borrowers were cast aside for unsophisticated home buyers. The result? Too many reckless loans to unqualified borrowers struggling to purchase overpriced homes.

And now? A glut of houses, home buyers who have become renters, huge losses on Wall Street and a struggling national economy.

tee when prices will recover. And keep in mind that, even as home prices fall, inflation is back. At just a modest 3% inflation rate, a dollar will lose about one-third of its value in ten years, further cutting into house values.

Worst-case scenario: Japan has seen residential real-estate prices fall 80% as it has suffered a real-estate depression since 1990 that, only in the last year or so, has shown signs of bottoming out, let alone recovering.

We should all hope that the problems in the United States play themselves out faster and less expensively. We'll see. . . .

THE OPPORTUNITY
OF A LIFETIME

I wish I were twenty-five again.

No, not for the obvious reasons, but because if the housing market runs the course it appears to be headed on, I could plan to buy my dream home at the threshold of my peak earning years for what will then look like next to nothing. Not since the darkest days of the Great Depression have young, *first-time home buyers* faced such an opportunity in the U.S. housing market.

Along with cheaper prices, today's twentysomethings are also likely to get a demographic break when it comes time for them to buy their houses. That's because the huge Baby Boom generation will be leaving a plentiful supply of homes as they age and die. It's a pattern of boom and bust that's always accompanied the Boomers, going back to the new schools built in the 1950s and shuttered in the 1970s.

With those long-term trends in mind, here's what a young adult and potential home owner needs to keep focused on:

- **There's no pressure to get into the housing market.** Don't listen to anyone who tells you that you must buy a house now. You can expect home prices to decline or remain stagnant well into the next decade. You have years to save your money and prepare to buy a home before prices will bottom out or start to tick up. Even if prices for the most distressed properties have already fallen 30% or more, the owners of other houses haven't capitulated yet. They still believe that, somehow, their house will not be affected by the downturn. They are wrong.

- **Save for retirement first.** The best investment anyone can make is to save in a 401(k) plan where you work. Starting your retirement savings early will pay off mightily in the end. A thousand dollars saved at age twenty-five in a typical retirement plan with an employer matching 50 cents on the dollar will be worth $22,500 at age sixty-five. That same $1,000 saved at age thirty will be worth just $16,000. If you concentrate on saving early in your career, you will have more money to spend later on your dream home.

OPPORTUNITIES EVERYWHERE

Median prices and values are still falling throughout much of the country. And remember: *median* means half the homes are cheaper still. Here's a *quick* run-through of Zillow's early 2008 house values in a few selected zip codes, compared to where they were in January 2006:

- 89081 (north Las Vegas): down 21%

- 90283 (suburban San Diego): down 15%

- 34639 (suburban Tampa): down 13%

- 32803 (Orlando): down 11%

- 60173 (suburban Chicago): down 5%

- **Develop the home-buying habit.** Set aside 28% of your salary—that's the rule of thumb for how much you should spend every month on a house payment. Spend no more than 20% of your gross salary on rent. Now, put the other 8% into a home-buying fund.

- **Pay your debts.** If you have student loans, plan to pay them off within ten years. Paying a $50,000 loan will cost about $6,700 a year. If you have credit card debt or auto loans (shame on you!), pay those off first. Pay the minimum on your student loan as you first tackle your high-interest consumer debts. Start by paying your highest interest debts first and work your way down to the lowest interest debts. And cut up your plastic.

- **Be frugal, live cheaply.** Live on just what you have left after savings, home expenses and debt payments. It's far easier to get by on just a few hundred dollars a month when you are in your twenties than it will be later. You don't have to live like a homeless person—give yourself plenty of treats—but keep your eye on the prizes: you want a secure old age, a home of your own and the freedom of living without debts. They all cost something.

A ROUGH ROAD AHEAD

As attractive as the declining market may turn out for first-time home buyers, it could be horrible for people who bought their first homes during the bubble. Like 1990s stock buyers who placed big bets on the likes of Pets.com or Webvan, these *early-cycle home buyers* could well see all their equity disappear as values fall.

Even buyers who played the game right—saving and making substantial down payments—could end up seeing that hard-saved equity vanish as house prices fall. Those who bought with no money down or with down payments of 10% or less face the unhappy prospect of making payments on

FORECLOSURE ISN'T THE ONLY OPTION

Foreclosure isn't the only way to get through a difficult time. Here's a list prepared by American Foreclosure Specialists, an Oklahoma company that helps home owners who have fallen behind on their payments and are facing foreclosure.

- **Reinstatement.** Pay the lender all of the back payments and fees to bring your mortgage current. This can be difficult and expensive.

- **Workout.** Negotiate to bring your loan back in good standing. Some examples: *Forbearance* is a temporary payment plan that holds payments in abeyance for a few months, usually due to death, divorce or a job loss. *Loan modification* involves renegotiating the terms of the loan, either to a new interest rate, reduced payments or, sometimes, forgiveness of some principal. With a *partial* claim, the lender will add the missed payments and fees to the principal.

- **Refinance.** Difficult in these times, but some lenders may be willing to refinance if you have sufficient equity.

- **Short sale.** Selling the house for less than the mortgage balance. The lender may be willing to take less than what you owe on the loan to avoid a costly foreclosure process.

- **Deed in lieu of foreclosure.** You give the home back to the lender and walk away. Some lenders may be persuaded not to report the transaction as a black mark on your credit report.

- **Bankruptcy.** Only a short-term fix. You will still be required to make your house payments.

mortgage balances that are higher than their homes are worth. No one wants to be paying $346,000 for something worth just $227,000. That's doubly true for home buyers who took out short-term ARMs and will be making higher monthly payments, too.

A WORLDWIDE WEB OF INFORMATION

As with so much of the world today, the Internet has thoroughly rewritten the rules about home buying, owning and selling. The housing information now available to anyone—everything from tax records to homes for sale—has greatly loosened the knowledge stranglehold that the professional real-estate community has long had over the home-buying public.

First, more and more county clerk offices are moving their vast warehouses of property information to the Web. You can find out just about whatever you need regarding past sales, owners and mortgages if you know how to access county property records.

Real estate is not yet the kind of free, open markets that you see in stocks, automobiles or consumer goods, but it's vastly more transparent today than it was even ten years ago.

Here's a brief rundown of some of the more useful commercial property-information sites on the Web. More Internet resources are listed in the bibliography.

Cyberhomes. Lots of home-valuation data, and good pictures of individual properties. *http://www.cyberhomes.com*

Eppraisal. Stronger for home sellers. *http://www.eppraisal.com*

Property Shark. Detailed; best for property investors; limited markets. *http://www.propertyshark.com*

Realtor.com. Real-estate industry's "multiple listing service" online. *http://realtor.com*

Trulia. Mainly geared to home shoppers. *http://www.trulia.com*

Zillow. Discussion boards and general real-estate information plus listings and market evaluation. *http://www.zillow.com*

- **Do the numbers.** Take the price you paid for your house and cut it by 25% ($300,000–25% = $225,000). That's about the hit that home owners can count on taking in this market—wiping out appreciation and, for recent buyers, their down payments, too. If at that 25%-off value, however, you still have substantial equity or are about even, then you will probably be able to ride out the storm, provided you have a steady job and you aren't facing unmanageably high interest resets.

- **Don't plan on moving for a while.** Fortunately, a house is not like a stock that you should dump when the value falls and the long-term trend is downward. As the saying goes, you can't live in a stock portfolio but you can live in your house. You may as well stay where you are rather than sell, take a loss and rent or buy into a declining market. Just be prepared to stay for a long time. Continue saving for the long term and accelerate your mortgage payments so you will increase your equity and reduce your long-term interest expenses. Every dollar you pay on your mortgage balance returns at least the interest you pay to borrow it. That may be the only return you see on your house for a long time.

- **Negotiate with your lender.** If you're struggling with your mortgage payments or falling behind and face the possibility of losing your house, there are a number of options that you can take to deal with the situation. For starters, don't try to handle the matter on your own. By all means, when you realize that you aren't going to be able to make your payment, contact your lender as quickly as possible to notify them of your predicament. Listen to what they have to say, but don't commit to any payback plan or program until you get professional assistance. You are at a great disadvantage dealing with the lender, who knows a lot more about this sort of business than you do. There are lawyers, state and local government offices and nonprofit organizations that specialize in helping distressed home owners with their mortgage problems. More and more state and local governments are setting up Web sites and hotlines to deal specifically with the problem. The Department of Housing and Urban Development *(http://www.hud.gov/offices/hsg/sfh/hcc/hcs.cfm)* provides links to state agencies and organizations that can help home owners.

- **Consider walking away.** Take a hard, unimpassioned look at your situation. If you lose your job, face onerous resets or the value of the house falls so far that you can't reasonably continue carrying the cost, giving up on the house may be your best plan. Don't let shame get in the way of a prudent financial decision; no well-managed corporation would continue throwing its good money after bad, and neither should you. To be sure, the psychological damage of losing your home is profound, but the damage of continuing to lose your money and sense of well-being will affect your finances and your psyche far longer. Remember: Default is a risk the lender chose to take when it made the loan to you in the first place. That risk was built into the interest rate that the lender charged and the private mortgage insurance (PMI) that you paid to ensure that the lender, not you, would be made whole. Yes, there will be damage to your credit rating, and yes, you will have difficulty buying a new house for a few years. But those will pass faster than it will take for your house to return to the price you agreed to pay and for you to get out from under a financial obligation that you can no longer afford.

RETHINKING THE MOVE UP

One of the nice things about owning rather than renting your home is that no one can make you move; no landlord will appear one day claiming his daughter or his nephew is moving to town and needs your apartment.

WASHINGTON TO THE RESCUE

Congress tried to address many of the problems in the housing market in the summer of 2008. It passed the Housing and Economic Recovery Act mainly to help troubled lenders—especially the struggling mortgage giants Fannie Mae and Freddie Mac, which were later taken over by the government.

But the law also includes a number of provisions—some of them very short term—that are aimed at the country's home buyers. Here are some of the high points:

Renegotiating mortgages. If you took out a mortgage on your primary residence before January 1, 2008, or your monthly payments are eating up too much of your income, you may be able to cancel your old mortgage and replace it with a new thirty-year, fixed-rate loan. The new mortgage amount would be no more than 90% of the current value of the house.

You are eligible for the new mortgage arrangement if your total monthly payment (principal, interest, taxes and insurance) are more than 31% of your household income.

There are plenty of hoops to jump through—and your lender isn't required to give you a better deal—but the new law might help buyers keep their houses.

Beware of some big drawbacks, however: You can't take out a home-equity loan for five years. Sell your home, and you will be required to share your appreciation with the government; sell in less than five years, and you will have to turn over all your gain. The program ends September 30, 2011.

Free money (sort of). If you bought your first home between April 9, 2008, and June 30, 2009, you might be eligible for a $7,500 tax credit on your 2008 taxes. (That's a dollar-for-dollar giveback. Pay $10,000 in taxes and you get back $7,500; pay $5,000 and get it all back plus an additional $2,500.) If your new home costs less than $75,000, you can claim a credit for only 10% of the price.

As always, there are a couple of catches: You have to pay the money back. The credit is essentially an interest-free loan that you will have to pay back over fifteen years, beginning with your 2010 taxes. Also, the credit phases out as your income rises. There's no credit if you are single and make $95,000 a year or are married and make $170,000.

Property tax deduction. Taxpayers who don't itemize may take up to a $500 deduction ($1,000 for married couples) for their state property taxes.

Higher reverse mortgages. The bill raises the amount that home owners can borrow with a reverse mortgage to $625,000. It also limits origination fees to 2% of a loan up to $200,000 and 1% beyond that—up to a limit of $6,000.

Bigger jumbo loans. The law redefines a jumbo loan as 115% of the local median home price—up to $625,000. That should help lower the borrowing costs of buyers in high-priced areas.

For *mid-cycle home buyers*—people who have been in the housing market for ten to twenty years and are now in their prime "move-up" years—not having to move on someone else's timetable is a blessing when values are falling and you may not be able to sell your existing home for as much as you had hoped.

Another big blessing: Unlike early-cycle buyers with little or no real ownership interest in their homes, mid-cycle buyers most likely have plenty of equity in their existing homes, from both price appreciation and principal payments. (Even in the lackluster housing markets of the Oil Patch states, prices have about doubled since 1990.) Of course, many mid-cycle buyers are in their second homes, so even if they do have a lot of equity—because they put down most of the sale proceeds from their first home into the second—they may still have many years of payments left on their mortgages.

In any case, a big overall value decline is not likely to have a significant impact on the financial well-being of a mid-cycle home buyer. What it should do, however, is give pause to hopes of moving up to a bigger house. Yes, all prices are relative and, yes, the price on the house you want to buy goes down just as the price you can get for your house goes down. You should still think twice before making that decision.

GIVE YOURSELF A PROPERTY TAX BREAK

Just as rising property values have a downside in rising property taxes, falling value can mean lower property taxes, but don't count on your local government to do the tax cutting for you. Anyone can appeal a property-tax assessment and trim a few hundred to a few thousand dollars from an annual tax bill. And your odds on getting some reduction are good.

Procedures differ by state and often by county, but here's a quick guide to cutting your bill:

Check the details. When you receive your annual tax bill, make sure that the description of the house is correct—that the assessor isn't hitting you for a four-bedroom house when you have only three. Check the time frame for appeals. In many counties you can appeal up to only sixty or ninety days after the tax bill goes out.

Size up your situation. Determine a valid market value for your house. Go on Zillow or to your assessor's Web site and see what other comparable houses have sold for recently. Check out what the neighbors are paying in property taxes.

File an appeal. Most counties will include an appeal form with your annual bill. If not, go to the assessor's site or call to find out how the procedure is handled in your locale. You will probably need to show the assessments on at least three comparable properties.

Keep fighting. If your initial appeal is turned down, you will probably be able to appeal that to the taxing agency's own appeals board. This will require you to make a court-like appearance. Work up your best presentation performance. Bring pictures. Bring evidence. Keep it brief.

- **Cash is king.** If you have the cash to buy a new house without selling your existing one, you are in a good position to move up—you will be able to drive a very good bargain and get your move-up home at a big markdown. If you need to sell your house in order to buy a new one, though, you have more problems. The last thing you want is to get caught in a daisy chain of buyers and sellers all hoping for one new buyer to step in: the Howells have agreed to sell to the Skipper, but he can't move because he's waiting to get his money from Ginger, who's trying to close her deal with the Professor, who's on the hook until Mary Ann can sell her place. You never want to be in a situation where everything depends on Gilligan.

- **Watch the trade up.** Likewise, you don't want to be caught trading up—and taking on more debt—on an asset that's declining in value. If you can't make a great deal—in most areas 30% or more off the bubble-era value—you shouldn't move. You don't want to jeopardize what equity you have built up by putting it into another house that may not go up for years. Better to bank that money in your retirement plan and pay down your existing mortgage.

- **Reconsider where you are.** You may also want to take a look at better using the space in your existing home to make the most of what you have. Many people want to move up for more space, when the kids become teenagers, for instance, and need a new bedroom or extra bathroom. But do you really need to move?

Look at it this way: despite today's smaller families, the size of houses has increased substantially in the past sixty years—from 1947's 750-square-foot Levittown suburban dream to the 2,300-square-foot mini-mansion of today.

Much of that bulking up is, literally, just air. It's bigger room volume that you can rearrange to better fit your needs. The second bedroom of the Levittown cape your grandparents bought in 1947 was 96 square feet (8 feet by 12 feet), and they managed to raise a couple of kids in it. (Think Wally and Beaver sharing a bedroom until Wally went off to college.) In today's homes, that second (and third and often fourth) bedroom is typically about 154 square feet.

I don't want to sound like a miserly spoilsport here; I like nice, big houses as much as the next guy, but we're talking about a world where the financial rules have changed, and you must change with them.

Before you go shopping for a new house, evaluate the space you already have. Generally, you can rearrange non-load-bearing walls in a house into new room configurations and even add a new bathroom for a fraction of the time and cost of moving or a major renovation.

Need a new bedroom? Can the one the kids are already sharing be divided? What about walling off the dining room you haven't used since Thanksgiving 1998? How about subdividing your "master suite" and swapping it for the kids' bedroom?

A new bathroom? What about the walk-in closet? Is the plumbing situated so that the closet could be converted to a bath? Or how about changing the laundry room into a bath and putting stacked washer-dryer units in a closet instead?

And do you need to move because your stuff has filled every closet, the utility room and the garage? Maybe you need less stuff.

PROTECT WHAT YOU HAVE

For many *home owners* and *late-cycle buyers,* the down market poses a big problem: If you have been planning on your home appreciation to fund a substantial part of your retirement and buy yourself a new downsized home in a retirement community, you are looking at a lot less money than you probably had hoped for. That's why it's bad planning to count on your house as a major component of your retirement fund.

IF YOU MUST SELL . . .

If job or life circumstances leave you no alternative but to sell in this market, here are some suggestions:

1. **Price it cheaply.** And do it when you put the place up for sale. Don't let the house hang around on the market as you gradually lower the price. Forget what you think the house should be worth or what it was worth three years ago. That's not what it's worth today.

2. **Don't wait around.** Don't try to wait out the market. That's what hundreds of other sellers are doing. You want your place sold. The best way to make sure that happens is to put it up for sale.

3. **Get a top real-estate agent.** This is no time to quibble over a couple of percentage points of commission. Hire the best, most aggressive selling agent (a.k.a. "listing agent") you can find. And offer her a bonus if she sells the house in thirty days or at your asking price.

4. **Clean it up and fix it up.** No buyer wants to see a house cluttered with other people's things, even yours. They want to imagine their stuff. Leave enough furniture to make the place look livable, but put stuff in storage. And give the place a new paint job and a general sprucing up. Imagine that buyers are taking your house out on a date. You want it to make a good impression.

5. **Promote. Promote. Promote.** Don't rely on the agent to do all the marketing work. Make sure your house is on all the real-estate Web sites, in the newspaper, your company's newsletter, even the bulletin board at the supermarket. Consider putting the house on eBay or Craigslist.com. You can't get too crazy.

6. **Take the offer.** If any qualified buyer comes in with a reasonable offer, be prepared to accept it. Don't squirrel the deal by digging in your heels over a few dollars. Negotiate, of course, but recognize that the buyer has a lot more clout than you do. Remember: your house is worth only as much as someone is willing to pay for it.

If overall housing prices fall 20%, your $500,000 house is going to be worth just $400,000, if you can find a buyer. Yes, your $200,000 golf course villa is going to be worth $160,000, but the $300,000 nest egg you planned to have will now end up being just $240,000. That's quite a hit to take just as you are retiring.

For those who have been in the housing market since at least the mid-1980s, the market is most unlikely to eat away more than just a few years of price appreciation (great years though they were!). And even if you are on your second or third house, you probably have a substantial ownership interest because you used your equity and appreciation from previous houses to buy your existing house.

What do you do now? Your main objective is to "monetize" your house. That's a clunky financial term for "convert into money" or to tap some or all of your home equity for cash. We'll go into a lot more detail in chapter 7 about various ways to get money out of the house, but for now we're going to concentrate on the best options in this market.

- **Become a banker.** Credit's tight, so potential home buyers may not be able to get loans from traditional lenders. If you own your home free and clear, then you could sell the house and carry the first mortgage yourself. There are risks to that—your buyers could default—but the upside can be considerable. Not only will the mortgage provide you a very nice monthly income, but you will be able to ask, and get, a higher price because you've foregone the hassles of dealing with a lender. And because you will be able to make the loan cheaper and easier than a traditional lender, you can require a higher interest rate for your troubles. You will have to buy your new home with other money, either savings or a loan, but you will have much improved cash flow. Here's a plus: if the buyer does default, you'll end up with your house, which you can sell again. One more thing: you'll need a good real-estate lawyer to set up everything.

- **Become a landlord.** You can turn your home into a rental property, creating income and earning some nice tax benefits for yourself. If you own your house and are no longer making mortgage payments, you will have considerable flexibility setting the rents and a significant competitive advantage over other landlords who have loans to pay. If you choose, you can also take out a new mortgage on the existing property to buy your new home; that way your tenants in effect buy your new home for you with their rent payments on the old property. If you plan to move a long way—say from New Jersey to Florida—you will want to hire a property manager to operate the place and deal with the tenants.

- **Stay where you are.** How much golf can you really play? Since the market is forcing you to rethink retirement plans, this is a good time to reconsider the whole idea of moving away from the community where you raised your family and built a lifetime network of friends and contacts. Homeowners can monetize their houses without selling them with home-equity loans, lines of credit or reverse mortgages. A home-equity loan is a traditional loan that puts a fixed sum in your bank account, which you pay back over time. A credit line is a loan that you must pay back, too, but it's an excellent emergency fund that, unlike a traditional home-equity loan or a refinanced "cash-out" mortgage, you can tap only when you need the extra money. A reverse mortgage, available to home owners age sixty-two and over, is a loan that you don't have to repay until you stop living in the house. And if you just have to escape winter, you can rent a place in Florida for three months of the year.

CHAPTER 3

MANAGING YOUR BIGGEST DEBT

I don't like to pay for the same real estate twice.
— GEORGE C. SCOTT
AS GENERAL GEORGE S. PATTON JR.
(*Patton,* screenplay by Francis Ford Coppola and Edmund North)

When movie stars, CEOs or billionaire hedge-fund managers pay millions of dollars for Malibu beach houses or Tribeca lofts, they don't buy their new homes the same way that the other 99% of us do.

Very rich people usually pay cash for their homes, often spending just a tiny portion of their net worth. They may borrow the purchase money for a short term—for a few months until they sell another house or investment property or sell some stocks or other holdings. But it's a rare multimillionaire indeed who goes through the lengthy process of qualifying for a mortgage, filling out the endless forms, photocopying paycheck stubs and all the other tedious, intrusive, soul-sapping financial dance steps that lenders may require of people who work for salaries. And it's unheard of among the upper crust to commit to thirty years of monthly payments and paying twice the value of their home in interest.

Like the rest of us do.

Of course, the most important financial decision that any home buyer makes is how much he or she is going to pay for a house. Number two on the list? How to pay for it.

That's because managing your biggest asset is really all about managing your biggest debt.

For most of us, they go hand in hand. Not many people reading this book have $300,000 or $400,000 in cash or stocks sitting around. If you do have that kind of money, it's probably already committed to funding your retirement or your kids' educations.

So, we go to a bank, a mortgage broker or an online lender to borrow more money than most of us have seen in one place in our entire lives. It's a daunting, sobering and numbingly expensive experience. A traditional thirty-year mortgage will end up costing you much, much more than the nominal price of the house in interest alone, often doubling the price of the house before the first property-tax bill is ever paid, before one coat of paint is applied or one new kitchen cabinet is installed.

It should go without saying that managing the mortgage— reducing the costs of borrowing wherever you can—is fundamental to the home-buying process and significantly enhances the investment value of a property. It should go without saying, but, as you'll see, it's home-owning advice that's rarely followed.

WHY A MORTGAGE ISN'T SUCH "GOOD" DEBT

You will often hear that mortgage debt is "good debt." Yes it is, but only in the broadest sense of the word. It's good debt because borrowing two or three times your annual salary to buy a home is better than going on a credit card binge or borrowing to take an around-the-world cruise on the *Queen Mary 2*.

But no debt can truly be considered good if it doesn't buy an income-producing asset that will cover the borrowing costs, pay back the principal and produce a profit. That's something the home-buying industry never addresses in its constant pitches to the public—and for good reason.

In business, a corporation may borrow $500 million to build a factory, but it doesn't make that commitment unless it's reasonably certain the new factory will produce enough cars or computers to pay back the lenders, to cover all costs to build, own and operate the factory, to pay the workers and to make a profit. On Wall Street, a sophisticated investor might take on the risk of borrowing to buy a hot stock, but he's betting that the price of that stock will shoot up so he can pay back the loan by selling some or all of it quickly enough that interest payments won't devour the profits. A landlord is likely to borrow to buy an apartment building, but his tenants pay the loan with their rent.

There's nothing comparable for a home buyer as houses don't pay for themselves in the same way that factories, stock investments or investment properties do. A typical single-family home doesn't produce income and, even during the kind of rocketing price run-ups we saw during the real-estate bubble, it won't increase in value quickly enough to offset most of the expenses of owning it.

This is important: A home doesn't pay for itself. You pay for it.

The costs of owning a home—the ongoing monthly mortgage-interest payments, maintenance, taxes and improvements, as well as the repayment of the loan principal—can be met only with the income of the owner or, long after the money's been spent, from the proceeds of a sale. A smart home buyer, then, must minimize mortgage debt as best he or she can in order to limit the overall costs of home buying.

BORROWING 101: AMORTIZATION

Amortization is a big word that describes how loans are accounted for, and it's important to understand how it works so you can understand how you pay off your mortgage.

Simply put: in an amortized loan, you pay interest on an ever-declining balance.

If you borrow $100,000 for thirty years at a *fixed rate* of 6.5% a year, your monthly payment is $632.07—that's a combination of interest and principal that will allow you to pay off the loan in 360 months. The first month, when you owe the full $100,000, $541.67 of your payment is interest and $90.40 is principal. (If you do the math, you can see the connection between the payment and the quoted interest rate; $541.67 $\times$ 12 = $6,500.04. That's 6.5% of $100,000.)

When the second month's payment is due, you owe only $99,909.60. But you write a check for the same $632.07 that you paid the first month. Now, however, $541.18 of your total is interest, and $90.89 is principal. In the next month, your loan balance is $99,818.71. It goes down every month, with the portion allotted to interest declining as the portion allotted to principal increases.

It's not until the twentieth year of the payback period (the 233rd month, in fact) that your check pays more principal than interest.

With an *adjustable rate,* the thirty-year amortization period remains the same, but the interest portion of the payment changes. In a one-month adjustable-rate mortgage, your payment can change month to month like a credit card, depending on the interest rates prevailing in international money markets, the benchmark (such as Treasury bond rates or the LIBOR— London Inter-Bank Offered Rate) your loan is pegged to and the specific terms of your loan agreement. Start with $100,000 at 6.5%, and the payment is the same $632.07, with the same interest-principal split. In the next month, if your loan rate rises to 7%, you will owe $582.81 of interest on the $99,909.60 balance.

Here's where adjustable-rate loans can get tricky. Some loans let you vary your payment to pay the extra interest (write your check for $664.71) while others hold the monthly payment steady and add the extra interest to your principal. That's called *negative amortization,* and it's something you want to avoid as you end up paying interest on interest.

Interest-only loans are not amortized at all. You have a low monthly payment because you pay only interest—$541.67 on a $100,000 loan—but there is no reduction of the principal. Most interest-only loans require a "balloon" payment of the total balance after five or ten years; some will convert to amortized loans after a few years.

MORTGAGE MANAGEMENT

Your primary mortgage is your number one home-owning expense. Fortunately, it's one of the very few expenses that you can do something about.

In fact, how you go about managing it could well mean the difference between making or losing money on your biggest asset. Even though you're not likely to ever be a movie star or run a multibillion-dollar hedge fund, there are a few lessons those people can teach you about buying a house.

Here are some broad principles to keep in mind:

- **Your mortgage should fit with *all* your dreams.** The more you pay for your house, the less you are devoting to your other financial goals. Debts should help you meet your goals, not get in the way of them. Never let yourself get in a position where you must decide whether to pay your house note or pay into your retirement plan or start your own company or save for your children's education. Most people have long-term dreams—including owning a home—but you shouldn't plan to shortchange one dream to achieve another. Allocate your income to meet all your financial goals.

- **It's real money.** Too many home buyers get carried away when they are shopping and dealing with dollar figures so far above their day-to-day experience. When you are getting ready to buy a house and take out a $300,000 loan, it's very easy to fold in another $10,000 here for a deluxe master bath upgrade or $15,000 for the finished garage-workshop. To paraphrase a once-famous senator: "Ten thousand here, ten thousand there and pretty soon you're talking real money." Every dollar you borrow you pay back two or three times. An extra $10,000 comes to $63 a month, enough to take the kids for burgers and a movie—forever.

- **Don't confuse mortgage payments with savings.** Mortgage payments are not a form of "enforced savings," despite what you may be told by your friends and the home-buying industry. Saving is saving; it's not spending. Gradually paying down your mortgage principal is gradually repaying a debt. And in today's housing market, you can't count on home-value appreciation to pay you a bonus on your equity. Over the years, inflating home values will rarely outpace the cost of long-term borrowing and other home-owning expenses.

- **Pay off your mortgage as quickly as you can.** The best way to manage any debt is to pay it. Making additional payments on your mortgage-loan principal reduces how much interest you pay and, as a result, more of every regular fixed monthly payment goes to principal, too. If you have to stretch to buy your house, stretch by paying principal, not interest. In the long run, you will see a greater return and increase in your net worth through a combination of speedy mortgage-debt reduction and prudent investing and saving.

There's no way I can tell you in this book what the best mortgage loan is for you. Only you know your dreams and how much money you have to achieve them. But no matter your particular case, you can apply these principles in your decision making and use them to evaluate your choices. They'll help you as you start sorting through this complicated mess that sure seems like high finance to most of us.

It wasn't always this way. Today's labyrinth of options is a relatively new phenomenon.

THE CHANGING GOALS
OF HOME BUYERS

When your grandparents bought their home during the great post–World War II housing boom, they probably had only one type of mortgage to choose from—a fixed-interest-rate loan made by a local bank or savings-and-loan that required a level payment every month for thirty years. Early on, each monthly check went to a big interest payment and a tiny bit of principal.

Over the years, as Grandpa's income increased, he and the other ex-GIs and their brides were thrilled to see that the monthly check consumed less and less of their incomes. There was extra money then, for vacations, for new appliances, for new cars. And ever so slowly, the interest portion of the check declined while the principal increased. And each check brought a big bonus. They were building equity—ownership—because as they paid down the mortgage principal they gradually acquired more and more of the property. As a bonus, the value of the house, their biggest asset, also increased. The perfect "two-fer" deal.

Your grandparents probably didn't see themselves as rich, but they were, by any definition, much, much wealthier than they had been when they started out and, most likely, much wealthier than they ever expected to be.

Grandma and Grandpa paid dutifully every month until one day, they wrote their 360th mortgage check. It may be hard to imagine today, but Americans used to have a big party when that day came. Grandma and Grandpa invited the cousins, the neighbors, maybe even the retired bank loan officer to a mortgage burning. They would, quite literally, take the promissory note—stamped "PAID"—and put a match to it. After thirty years, they finally owned their home "free and clear."

Your grandparents were quite likely to be the first people in their families to ever own their own home. And that home-owning family tableau remains a strong image with many Americans, reinforced every Christmas season with the TV airing of the Jimmy Stewart–Donna Reed–Lionel Barrymore movie *It's a Wonderful Life.* Good, solid, middle-class people climbing the socioeconomic ladder by their own hard work, frugality and perseverance.

It also bears little resemblance to modern home buying.

There are still thirty-year, fixed-rate mortgages, of course, and they are still very popular with buyers. But there are as many different types of mortgages today as there are buyers.

That's because today's buyers don't tend to view a home as a lifelong commitment. Similarly, a mortgage is less a debt to be paid off over a long time as it is a financial instrument to be used and discarded as life and economic events allow. Today, a typical family may have three or more houses over a thirty-year period, and mortgages can be shed and refinanced as often as interest rates and circumstances change.

That mind-set has pluses and minuses. On the positive side, families can easily move up to bigger, nicer houses in better neighborhoods as their incomes grow. But the big downside to that is that families take on ever higher amounts of mortgage debt as they move up and take out new mortgage loans. So, the mortgage burning happens much less often—about one-third of retirees today have mortgage payments—and the "free and clear" moment is postponed indefinitely.

This is largely the result of a big change in home-owning and mortgage-borrowing practices that came in the inflationary 1970s, when the Baby Boomers, the parents of today's first-time home buyers, were just entering the housing market.

House prices were way up—what was then an astounding $50,000 for a starter home. But interest rates were out of control. The average thirty-year mortgage-interest rate in 1975 was 9.05% and rising. In 1981, it peaked at 16.63%!

TALKING THE TALK

The vast majority of home mortgages fall into two broad categories, conforming and non-conforming loans.

Conforming mortgage loans are made in accordance with guidelines established by the two big mortgage guarantors taken over by the government in 2008—Fannie Mae and Freddie Mac (both better described by their former, more formal names, Federal National Mortgage Association and Federal Home Loan Mortgage Corp., respectively).

When you borrow money to buy a house, you contract with a "loan originator," a local bank or a huge national corporation such as Countrywide or Washington Mutual, but most of them don't hold on to your mortgage for long. They sell your loan and others to Fannie Mae or Freddie Mac, which in turn, package large groups of loans together and then resell them in the bond market as "mortgage-backed securities." Those are bought mainly by large institutional investors such as insurance companies, pension funds and foreign governments. The market for mortgage securities was the epicenter of the credit crisis of 2007–2008. It essentially stopped operating.

You may sometimes see conforming loans called "conventional" loans. That's not totally accurate, but no one will deny your application if you use the terms interchangeably.

Jumbo or *non-conforming* loans are used to buy more expensive houses; their requirements are outside the Fannie Mae and Freddie Mac guidelines. They, too, are packaged and sold in the bond market. Because jumbo loans carry a higher risk, interest rates generally run a half percent or so higher than for conforming loans. Likewise, lenders may charge higher origination fees and require down payments that are a greater percentage of the purchase price of the home.

There is also a third category of loans that became more important after the credit crisis. *Government-guaranteed* loans are backed by the Federal Housing Authority (FHA) and the Department of Veterans Affairs (VA). Those agencies don't make the loans themselves, but they guarantee loans made by traditional lenders. Interest rates can be higher than for other types of loans.

FHA loans generally are for lower-income individuals. They require at least a 3% down payment, and loan ceilings vary from region to region: more for a single-family home in New York, less in Des Moines. For more information see: *http://fha.mortgageloanplace.com.*

VA loans—for former members of the armed services—had their heyday in the post–World War II boom, when GIs could buy homes with nothing down. See: *http://www.homeloans.va.gov.*

First-home buyers, who are essential for the housing pyramid to keep growing, were hard-pressed to afford the high payments. One solution that lenders came up with was the widespread introduction of adjustable- or variable-rate mortgages, which promised the young married Boomer couples lower payments in the early years of home buying. The adjustable-rate mortgage was so attractive not just because it made buying a home more affordable, but also because not everything about inflation was so bad, especially for young people just starting out with dreams a lot bigger than their salaries.

"Nominal" incomes (the actual numbers on a paycheck, not accounting for the declining value of inflationary dollars) were rising along with prices, so the Boomers figured out that if they borrowed a lot of money today they would pay it back later with much cheaper dollars. And they would be able to afford the adjustable-rate mortgages' higher interest costs down the line because they could expect their salaries to inflate along with everything else.

Furthermore, income-tax brackets weren't indexed to inflation then, so the government's mortgage-interest tax deduction was more valuable than it is today. A young, college-educated, two-earner family in 1981, for instance, could easily land in the 50% bracket with the government then subsidizing half of their mortgage interest. After taxes, a $1,000 a month interest expense cost the couple just $500. (And this is when *all* interest payments were deductible—auto loans, college loans, even credit cards.)

Dealing with numbers like that, the Boomers quickly learned how to play the inflationary housing market: stretch to buy as much house as you can and put as little money down as possible, then sell and do it again . . . and again.

This plan worked well for the particular time and market, but it's not one you want to continue following today. We live in a much different housing market, interest rates are much lower, tax laws have changed, and incomes are not rising as fast.

What's the best way to manage your mortgage today? Let's start with the first question a new buyer needs to ask. . . .

FIXED OR ADJUSTABLE?

It depends. Do you live a fixed or an adjustable life?

If, like Grandma and Grandpa, you plan to live in your home for a lifetime, you will most likely want a fixed-rate mortgage. It's the vanilla of home loans.

The traditional, thirty-year, fixed-rate loan is simple to understand and simple to keep track of. Every monthly check is the same, with the amount of interest you pay declining with each payment. The steady month-in-and-month-out expense is great for budgeting, and it's always good to know that there is at least one major, unavoidable bill in your life that doesn't go up when everything else does. When home-buying advocates extol the virtues of buying, they usually cite the advantage of the steady thirty years of payments. You can't beat it.

Today's rates on thirty-year loans are relatively low, certainly when compared to the double-digit rates Baby Boomers remember from the 1970s and '80s, but they are not significantly out of line with rates throughout most of the post–World War II era.

Not all fixed-rate loans extend for three decades. Interest rates are generally lower, but monthly payments are higher with fifteen-, twenty- or twenty-five-year loans. The shorter loan

PAYING A $300,000 LOAN

Years	Interest rate	Monthly payment	Total interest
15	6.00	$2,532	$155,683
20	6.15	$2,175	$222,081
30	6.50	$1,896	$382,637
40	6.75	$1,810	$568,836

periods mean much lower overall interest payments, which means you spend less money by paying off your house faster. Even before the real-estate bubble, some lenders had begun offering lower monthly payments with extended forty-year fixed-rate loans, featuring lower monthly payments than the standard thirty-year but higher interest rates.

INTEREST RATE VERSUS APR

Mortgage loans carry a quoted interest rate (that's the one you see in the ads) and a slightly higher rate called the APR or "annual percentage rate." Stating the APR is required by federal lending regulations.

The APR more accurately portrays the total cost of borrowing, although it does it in a rather clunky way. The APR is the basic interest rate plus the costs of the upfront fees and points that go into acquiring the mortgage. Those are paid when you get the money, but the APR is written as if the costs are spread out over the term of the loan.

What the APR doesn't tell is what you will pay each month and how much of your payment will go to interest and to principal. That's figured with the quoted interest rate.

So what's not to like?

Remember that even the good old thirty-year, fixed-rate loans are really, really expensive. The forty-year loans are downright outrageous. Not by the month, but over the long haul.

That's because it takes a long time and a lot of interest to pay off a thirty- or forty-year note. A family with a $300,000, thirty-year home loan will end up paying $382,000 above that in interest before their mortgage burning. (Yes, the government subsidizes that with the mortgage-interest tax deduction. Remember: the value of the deduction isn't nearly as great for average buyers as you may believe.)

In the early years of the thirty-year loan, the payback of the principal is excruciatingly slow. That didn't bother many bubble-era borrowers as long as home prices were rising rapidly, and they built ownership mainly through price appreciation rather than loan payoff. But without hefty price rises, long-term borrowers won't build up much equity in their homes unless they stretch themselves to make extra principal payments each month.

Look at the following graph. It shows the cumulative payments, broken out by interest and principal, on a $300,000 loan at 6.5% over thirty years. Total payments approach $700,000, with almost $400,000 in interest payments.

It's bad enough that interest payments on long-term loans are so expensive, but another big problem with long-term,

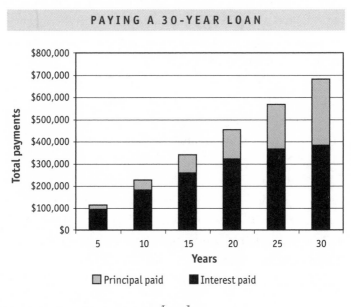

PAYING A 30-YEAR LOAN

fixed-rate mortgages is that they don't fit the way most home buyers live today. Most American home buyers move to a new house every five to seven years, long before they have made a significant dent in their loan balances.

Take another look at the graph: after five years, you have paid nearly $100,000 in interest but barely scratched the principal. Some savings account.

KNOW WHERE YOU'RE GOING

The Boomers' housing attitudes have prevailed, influencing home buyers across the country. If you are like your Boomer parents, you, too, may think of houses as just way stations along the road of an evermore prosperous life. Start with a small condo in the city, move up and out to a modest two-bedroom in a suburb when you start a family, move up again to a bigger, even more expensive, trophy house in a leafier suburb when the kids are older, and then, when the kids finish college, maybe back to a condo in the city or to a villa on a golf course in the Sun Belt.

That's an expensive choice of lifestyles, restarting the mortgage-debt clock with every move and never really building the kind of equity that you hope. But if it's the way you want to go, you need to make sure that your mortgage loans fit the way you intend to live.

For you, the "chocolate" flavor of mortgages—an adjustable-rate loan—may be the best choice, especially the types of loans that adjust after extended periods of five, seven or ten years of fixed payments. These are typically described as "5/1" or "7/1" or "10/1" ARMs, meaning they carry a fixed rate for the initial five or seven or ten years, and then adjust yearly after that. The initial interest rates can be as much as a full percentage below comparable fixed-rate loans, lower still if you are willing to pay substantial "discount" points when you first borrow the money.

POINTS VERSUS NO POINTS

Among the costs associated with taking out a mortgage is the genuinely odd practice of paying "upfront" points. It's not enough that lenders charge you regular interest on the money you borrow; many want to charge you even more for the privilege of letting you do business with them.

Imagine if the supermarket put a turnstile at the checkout and charged you a dollar just to go through the line to pay for your groceries.

Points are a percentage of the overall loan amount. One point (points are percentages of the total loan; 1 point = 1%, 2 points = 2%, etc.) of a $300,000 loan is $3,000; four points equal $12,000. As onerous as these fees may appear, don't dismiss the idea of paying points out of hand. If you know what you're paying, you can make points work in your favor by significantly lowering your house costs over the years.

First, there are two types of points, one bad, one good. Avoid *origination points* whatever you do. You really are paying at the checkout with these, as they often go to paying a mortgage broker's fee or covering the myriad charges and fees that home buyers face at closing. Further insult: origination points are not generally deductible unless they are specifically required to obtain the mortgage. If a lender or mortgage broker insists on origination points, then don't do business with them.

Discount points are a different animal. They are prepaid interest that lower the interest rate on your loan and cut the overall cost of the house. The difference in a monthly payment between a no-points mortgage and a points mortgage can be substantial, and the longer you plan on keeping your house the better for you. Plus, discount points are deductible in the year you take out the loan.

Example: A $300,000, thirty-year loan at 6.5% costs $1,896 a month. In the first year, you'll pay about $19,400 in interest and $3,350 in principal. Over ten years, you'll pay a total of $227,000—$181,000 in interest and $46,000 in principal.

But suppose you agree to pay four discounts points (4%) when you take out the loan and buy a 4.5% rate instead? Yes, $12,000 is a lot of money, but it will pay for itself many times over. That same $300,000 loan will now cost you just $1,520 a month. You will pay $4,840 in principal in the first year and just $13,400 in interest.

By the tenth year? Your total payments will reach just $182,000—about $122,000 in interest and $60,000 in principal. So your $12,000 upfront payment saved you $91,000. If your lender doesn't offer you discount points, ask about them.

Here's the clincher: Go to Jack Guttentag's terrific Mortgage Professor Web site (*http://www.mtgprofessor.com*) and look for the "Mortgage Points Calculator: Rate of Return on Fixed-Rate Mortgages" among his useful online calculators. Plug in all these numbers, and you'll see the ten-year rate of return on your $12,000 payment comes to almost 38%! That's a great investment anytime. And in this housing market, it's probably better than the house itself will do over the same period.

The bottom line: discount points are always a good deal if the cost of the points can be recouped with lower monthly payments and greater equity accumulation over the term you plan to keep the loan.

Steer clear, however, of loans with adjustment periods shorter than five years, and ignore the absurdly low "teaser rates" that you see in lenders' advertisements. Those rates rarely last much longer than it takes for the ink to dry on your loan agreement, and, like the foreclosed home buyers who are now renters again, you will be shocked when payments start rising dramatically before you even have all your moving boxes unpacked.

A typical such arrangement to avoid is a so-called 2/28 mortgage. The interest rate is fixed at a relatively low rate for the first two years but then floats for the next twenty-eight years. In many cases, that "reset" of the interest rate after two years leads to a monthly payment increase of 30% or more.

Always "worst case" the loan terms to see what will happen if you don't move as soon as you plan or if you get caught in a credit crunch that keeps you from refinancing. A 5.5% rate for five years is good, but will you be able to afford a 7.5% rate in year nine if your plans to sell or refinance don't pan out?

VARIATIONS ON THE BASIC THEMES

Within the fixed- or adjustable-rate loan menus are a number of variations. The selection can be frightening. A visit to the Web site of Countrywide Financial, the nation's top mortgage lender, searching for a $300,000 purchase loan for a house in Atlanta comes up with nearly thirty choices, ranging from the benchmark thirty-year fixed-rate loan to much more exotic offerings such as the "Pay Option ARM—1 Month," an "80/20—no down payment," even something called the "Credit Comeback Loan." And within those broad categories, there are even more choices. Points or no points. Interest only, ARM or fixed. One-month ARM. Ten-year ARM.

Citimortgage, a unit of Citibank, lists a dozen types of thirty-year fixed loans; a similar range of choices is listed under other loan options.

Which loan is *best*? Even experienced loan shoppers can be excused for finding all this too difficult to figure out. That's part of the reason people go to independent mortgage brokers, who are supposed to figure out what loan best fits the customer's needs.

That's fine, but a reasonably smart person can make sense of it all on his own, especially once he has determined how long he plans to hold on to the house. After that, it's really just a case of figuring which loan is cheaper over the term you intend to hold on to the house. Add up all the costs and monthly payments and determine how much the loan will cost you by the time you plan to move.

Are you going to stay in your place forever? Compare the various long-term loans to determine which one will be the easiest to pay off quickly, maybe a fifteen- or twenty-year fixed-rate loan is for you. Up and out when the kids head off for college? How about a 10/1 ARM? Flipping in a hot real-estate market where you plan to sell out in just a year or so? Consider an interest-only loan.

The important thing is to get a loan that fits your plans—that minimizes your costs and maximizes your return on the property—and avoid any loan that you don't easily understand.

Confronting the worst-case scenario before you buy can help you avoid the fate of the many home buyers who lost their homes as the bubble burst. They had stretched themselves just to buy their houses, relying on the low teaser rates for just a year or two. They were then unable to afford the new, higher payments that came when their rates reset; they were unable to refinance because their houses had not appreciated as they had hoped, and credit had tightened. In other words, they were doomed.

At the core of the foreclosed buyers' problems, however, was a fundamental misunderstanding of what an adjustable-rate loan is all about. Buyers should never rely on the lower monthly payments just to buy more house. The real financial advantage of an adjustable-rate mortgage is that you are borrowing at lower, shorter-term interest rates. So you get lower overall payments during the initial loan period while paying more principal each month.

For many borrowers, it's a great deal because you get to live in your house for just the length of time you planned for much less money than a fixed-rate mortgage would cost.

Consider next-door neighbors John and Steve, two middle managers who each took out $300,000 loans to buy identical houses five years ago. John got a 5.5% 5/1 adjustable-rate loan while Steve got a 6.5% fixed-rate mortgage. John's monthly payment is $1,703; Steve pays $1,896, almost $200 a month more.

Both John and Steve have the long-term goal of not having a mortgage payment at all when they retire in thirty years.

At thirty-five, both home buyers got big new jobs with big raises and decided to sell and move. Who's ahead? John, by a mile. His adjustable-rate loan balance is about $277,000, but Steve still owes $281,000. That may not sound like much of a difference, but John spent only about $79,500 on interest while Steve spent $94,600. So that's an $18,000 advantage to John.

Rest assured, however: the ARM lender gets his *and more* on the back end.

If John doesn't get that new job, or if he's caught in a real-estate market downturn and can't sell his house or refinance, he faces big jumps in his monthly house payments as his loan rate adjusts. That's not just because the loan rate itself rises, which it usually does. The term of the loan also changes. The first five years of the loan term were based on a thirty-year amortization. With the first payment of the sixth year, however, the payment will be based on a twenty-five-year term.

Let's say John's adjustable loan, which was 5.5% for thirty years with a $1,703 monthly payment, adjusts to a new rate of 6% figured on his new $277,000 balance with a twenty-five-year payback period. The new monthly payment? $1,785. That doesn't sound so bad.

But John has a 5/1 loan, meaning that the terms will readjust every year after the first five. (Fortunately, adjustable-rate loans have interest-rate "caps," limiting how much the rate can rise from year to year up to a top rate. In this example, we're using an annual cap of one-half of a percentage point and a 9.5% lifetime cap.)

FIXED VERSUS 5/1 ARM PAYMENTS

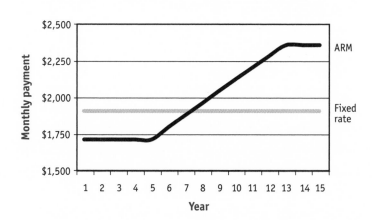

Let's say John's loan rate rises by another half percentage point the next year: Year seven's payment? $1,870 a month. Year eight? $1,953. By the thirteenth year of the loan, John could be paying $2,349 a month, 9.5% on a balance of $242,000.

Steve, with his plain vanilla fixed-rate 6.5% loan, looks smarter and smarter with each of John's rate adjustments. By the thirteenth year, Steve's loan balance will be about even with John's, but Steve will still be paying the same $1,896 a month.

And over thirty years? Steve will end up shelling out $682,000 to pay off his $300,000 loan; John will end up paying $98,000 more than that, the difference all in interest.

FIXED RATE VERSUS 5/1 ARM

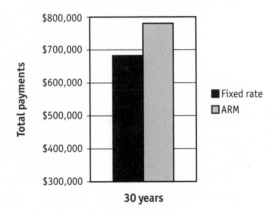

30 years

WHY IT PAYS TO PAY OFF YOUR MORTGAGE

Steve and most other people can find something else to do with $382,000 besides pouring it down a black hole of interest payments. Remember: interest is just rent you pay to a lender rather than a landlord.

When house prices were rising at 15% or 20% a year, there might have been an argument to be made for not paying a mortgage quickly. Property values were increasing so rapidly that mortgage debt could be viewed as a cheap and decreasing cost of ownership.

It's called leverage: a $375,000 house increasing in value at 20% a year could be expected to double in value in less than four years, and the original $75,000 down payment would grow to more than $400,000. With an upside like that, an extra $200 a month principal payment would be just an extra drop in an overflowing bucket. Why bother?

But in a stagnant or declining housing market, those drops add up. What happens if the value of the house increases just 3% a year—the basic rate of inflation?

After five years, the house would be worth $434,000. Steve, with his fixed-rate mortgage, would owe $281,000, despite having paid nearly $97,000 in interest over the period. Let's assume another $500 a month for maintenance, insurance, property taxes and other "I-have-to-pay-something" costs. Steve is now out another $30,000. Put another way, Steve has paid $127,000 for a $59,000 paper gain that, because of inflation, is really no gain at all.

The numbers are worse in a falling market. If the value of the house goes down just 1% a year for five years, it will be worth only $357,000. And Steve will have paid $127,000 for a loss of $18,000. And in the kind of market much of the country is facing now, Steve's house could lose 30% of its value—a huge paper loss of $112,500, including all of Steve's down payment. Worse still, Steve could wind up "upside down" in his house—carrying a loan balance that's greater than what the house is worth.

These are not the kinds of numbers that build a comfortable nest egg.

So what should Steve do?

First, he has to change his mind-set. His house is clearly not a very good savings vehicle. In fact, even if the house value is rising modestly, it's still costing Steve more money every month than he's making in appreciation. Who would hold on to a stock that costs more every month to own than it makes?

Steve has to control his costs, and the easiest, most effective expense for him to take charge of is his interest payment.

WHAT WOULD YOU DO WITH AN EXTRA $10,000?

Everyone from time to time gets a windfall—a bonus, an unexpected tax refund, an inheritance. It's a great feeling. But before you check out the cost of a week in Cancún or the lease on a new BMW, think about what that money could do for you.

If you decide to put your $10,000 into remodeling your bathroom, you will have a nice new bathroom, but your investment will return only about $8,500 if you sell your house in the next five years or so—if the housing market has recovered. Over thirty years, your new bathroom, which won't be so new anymore, will contribute little if anything to the resale value of your house.

If you can spot the next Google, you could roll the dice and buy $10,000 worth of stock. Then, watch it grow to more than $80,000 in only five years. But if you spot the next Pets.com, instead, you will have nothing.

A more prudent form of stock investing would be to put your $10,000 in a broad-market index fund that grows about 7% a year. It will be worth about $76,000 in thirty years.

Depending on how long you have had your mortgage, paying $10,000 toward your balance could save you up to $54,000 in interest payments and trim thirty-three months off a $300,000, 6.5%, thirty-year, fixed-rate mortgage.

Think like a financial pro for a moment. Which is better? Invest for 7% or pay 6.5%? With these numbers, it's virtually a wash, with a slight edge over the long haul to investing in the stock market rather than paying down the mortgage. With different investment returns, such as buying a $10,000, 4.75% certificate of deposit or putting it in a 3% money-market account, the mortgage pay down will do better for you.

Be on watch: as mortgage-interest rates rise or as ARMs reset higher, it is almost always going to be to your benefit to pay down principal.

Yes, he can go to city hall and get his property taxes lowered based on the declining value of the house; he can fire the lawn crew and cut the grass himself; he could even start carpooling and get rid of the second car he had to buy because he bought a house twenty-five miles from his office.

But the elephant in the great room is still his interest payment—$19,000 a year. That's what has to be cut if Steve wants to turn around his financial picture.

Steve's short-term solution is to refinance the mortgage. If he's lucky and rates have taken a turn south, he might get a 5.5% fixed-rate, thirty-year loan instead of his current 6.5%. Remember, his mortgage loan balance is $19,000 lower than it was five years ago, so Steve will be borrowing less money at a lower interest rate. He could get his monthly payment down from $1,896 to $1,595, a very nice savings.

Unfortunately for home buyers, the problem with most simple refinances is that they are short-term fixes. Most home owners refinance just to reduce their monthly payments, but they lose in the long term. That's because most people who refinance just restart the thirty-year mortgage clock. After refinancing, Steve will be $300 a month richer, but he will be no closer to actually owning his own home than he was five years ago. He'll still be facing thirty years of house payments, and he will be pushing his long-term goal—no mortgage at retirement—ahead five more years.

One solution? Refinance with a new twenty-five-year term rather than thirty years. If he does that, Steve's new monthly payment will be $1,726. He'll be paying $170 a month less and will stay on plan for his retirement.

As long as interest rates fall, Steve can repeat this process over and over, reducing his monthly costs and shortening loan terms while increasing the portion of his monthly payment that goes toward principal and keeping on his long-range plan. He can even do this by judiciously employing adjustable-rate loans with their even lower interest costs.

A LITTLE EXTRA GOES A LONG WAY

The easiest and best way to pay off your mortgage is to simply tack extra money to your monthly mortgage check. The advantage goes back to the way an amortized loan works: you pay interest on a declining balance, so the less principal you owe, the less interest you pay.

If you pay your note online through your bank or bill-paying service or with automatic withdrawals by the lender, you will probably want to add a fixed amount to your scheduled payment—an extra $100, or whatever. One common practice is to add one-twelfth of your scheduled payment to every check, thus making the equivalent of thirteen monthly payments a year. If you write paper checks, you can add a fixed amount or whatever you feel comfortable adding that month—$100 one month, nothing the next, $1,000 when your tax refund arrives.

Alternatively, some people just write a thirteenth check every year. Be sure to write "principal payment" on the check, or the bank may apply it to your next month's payment or to your escrow account.

Some lenders have formalized rapid payoffs with "biweekly" mortgages, in which you pay half a month's payment every two weeks, making twenty-six half payments a year instead of twelve full payments.

Properly set up, a biweekly mortgage can mean substantial savings in time and money, cutting $157,000 of interest and about six years from a $300,000, thirty-year loan.

Be careful. Read the fine print and do the math. There is usually an extra fee to set up a biweekly schedule. And some lenders don't apply the extra principal until the end of the year, negating much of the advantage of the early payment.

But rates will fall only so far. Interest rates hit their forty-year nadir in 2003, when the average thirty-year fixed loan rate fell to 5.23%, fueling the housing bubble and unleashing the greatest wave of refinancings in history. Barring a general economic meltdown, however, we're unlikely to see rates fall lower than they did then.

For Steve, subduing his debt now means he's going to have to take another tack. First, he's going to have to start thinking long term. He'll have to forget about cutting his month-to-month housing costs and look, instead, at cutting his long-term interest costs.

And the only way to do that is to pay down principal.

In the first year of his new twenty-five-year, 5.5% loan, Steve will pay $15,300 interest and $5,400 principal. Year two: $15,000 and $5,700. Over the twenty-five-year term, he will still pay more than $236,000 of interest.

To cut that figure even more, Steve should take that $170 a month he's saving with his new loan and keep paying it to his lender. If he does that, he'll shave more than four years from his loan term—pushing his retirement goal that much closer—and cut an additional $46,000 of interest.

In other words, paying the same fixed $1,896 a month that he has been paying all along, Steve will end up saving $96,000, cutting his interest payments from $382,000 to $288,000 and owning his home free and clear four years earlier than he had originally planned.

But that's not his only option. Steve could accomplish virtually the same dollar savings while paying off his loan even faster—without refinancing. How? By simply adding his monthly income-tax savings to his monthly mortgage payment. Steve's mortgage-interest tax deduction saves him $183 a month. (Remember, the actual tax savings to a home buyer is only the difference between the mortgage-interest deduction and the standard deduction—$2,200, or $183 a month, in the first year in this case.) If Steve uses that money to pay his principal—

PAY-OFF PENALTIES

Be wary if a lender offers you a loan with a "pre-payment penalty." That's extra money the lender will charge if you choose to pay off your loan earlier than the agreed upon term. Lenders usually charge penalties to keep you from refinancing the loan within the first few years, but some will want to hit you up even if you sell.

Risky borrowers usually get hit with a double-whammy of high interest rates and prepayment penalties that can be as high as 5% of the total loan if you refinance in the first year or two. So a typical sub-prime borrower could face an interest reset to 10% or more and a 5% penalty if he wants to refinance to a lower rate. Just say, "No thanks." No one needs to buy a house that much.

That warning made, however, there are instances when borrowers with good credit scores might want a loan with a penalty. Some lenders may offer good credit risks a lower interest rate in exchange for a three- to five-year commitment, charging 2% or 3% of the total loan if you refinance during the period. A quarter-point rate reduction can mean a $100 a month or so savings on a $300,000 loan, so if you plan to stay a long time it might be worth it. Borrowers with good credit are in the best position to negotiate, so ask when you first approach a lender.

raising his monthly payment to $2,079 or making a single annual payment of $2,200—Steve will save about $97,000 in interest and pay off his loan in the twenty-fourth year of his loan, when he's just fifty-four years old.

Adding an additional $400 a month—which would bring Steve's monthly payment to about what his neighbor John will pay when his adjustable-rate loan reaches its top limit—will save Steve $160,000 and give him a shot at retirement at age fifty-one.

PAYING A FIXED-RATE LOAN EARLY

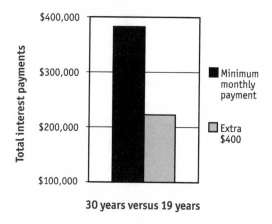

30 years versus 19 years

PAYING OFF AN ARM

What about John? How can someone who is stuck in a stagnant market with an ARM better manage the mortgage?

Once again: pay it off. An ARM is great through the initial period, but John probably doesn't want to face too many rate resets as the principal portion of each monthly payment declines while the interest rate rises. Beginning in the seventh or eighth year of a 5/1 ARM term, John, unlike fixed-rate Steve, will be paying more interest, not less, with each monthly check.

If interest rates are in John's favor—that is, if they are still significantly below the top adjusted rate on his existing loan— then John's best strategy is to refinance to a fixed-rate mortgage. Because he put 20% down and has been paying lots of principal through the initial period of the loan, the property will probably qualify for a new loan even if its market value has declined 5% or 10%. It may be more difficult if the market has fallen further, but with John's substantial equity in the house and an overall lousy housing market, certainly his primary lender would be predisposed to work with him to make a new deal happen on terms acceptable to both.

(John, by the way, is not facing the same problems that whacked foreclosed home buyers in the sub-prime mortgage crisis. More than just interest-rate resets precipitated the melt-down, including careless lenders making bad loans to unqual-ified borrowers to buy overpriced houses.)

That said, when John converts to a fixed-rate loan, he should be prepared to pay more each month than he has been. His $1,703 monthly payment on his 5/1, $300,000, 5.5%, thirty-year ARM loan could end up becoming a $2,047 pay-ment on a fixed $277,000, 7.5%, twenty-five-year loan.

But what if John can't convert to a fixed-rate loan? What if interest rates have skyrocketed to the levels of the early 1980s? What if the house value has declined so much that it won't qualify for a new fixed-rate loan? What if lenders just aren't making new loans? Well, John's top interest rate might look pretty good in any of those dire cases.

First, John had better be prepared to do some serious arithmetic.

It's not as easy to pay off an ARM early as with a fixed-rate loan because every time the monthly payment resets, the term of the loan also resets. So the new payment is computed on the years remaining of the initial thirty-year term. Think of it this way: the rate adjusts, but the thirty-year term of the loan is fixed.

On John's 5/1 ARM, the payment in the sixth year will be based on the remaining twenty-five years of the initial term; the payment in the fifteenth year will be computed on a fif-teen-year term.

It's complicated, but John *can* pay it off early. First, he has to use the initial low interest rate to his advantage so that when the monthly payments do reset, he both keeps his payment manageable and increases his extra principal payment each time the interest rate resets.

We already know that John was way ahead of Steve over the first five years, paying about $200 less every month and chip-ping into his principal faster while paying less interest. But what if John had taken that savings and applied it to his mortgage from day one? His savings would have compounded mightily.

If he pays the same monthly note as Steve—$1,896—he will make an additional $13,000 dent in his loan balance. At the end of the fifth year, John would owe just $264,000. His required payment in the sixth year, after the adjustment to 6%, would be $1,702. But if John continues to pay $1,896 and then includes an additional $200 (total extra payment = $393), he'll write checks for $2,096 a month through the sixth year and end up with a loan balance of $254,000—that's $18,000 ahead of where he'd have been paying just the required minimums.

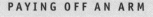

PAYING OFF AN ARM

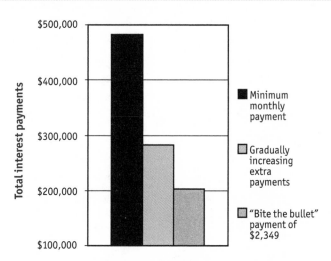

In the seventh year, John's rate will adjust up to 6.5%, the term will shorten to twenty-four years, and he will be required to pay a minimum of $1,747. If he adds another $100 to his extra payments (now totaling $493), he'll pay $2,196 a month and end the year with a balance of $238,000. If John follows this plan and adds another $100 of extra payment in the eighth year and another $100 in the ninth year, his monthly payments will max out at $2,396—just $50 more than his payment would be at his top interest rate. John will save $200,000 in interest and pay off midway through the twenty-second year. That would give John, like Steve, a shot at retirement in his mid-fifties. (And if his interest rates decline—don't hold your breath—John will save even more and pay off his loan.)

Here's a table that traces one way John can accelerate his loan payoff:

			Minimum	Extra	Total	
Year	Interest	Principal	payment	principal	payment	Balance
						$300,000
1	$16,340	$4,101	$20,441	$2,316	$22,756	$293,583
2	$15,978	$4,462	$20,442	$2,316	$22,756	$286,805
3	$15,596	$4,845	$20,443	$2,316	$22,756	$279,644
4	$15,192	$5,249	$20,444	$2,316	$22,756	$272,079
5	$14,765	$5,675	$20,445	$2,316	$22,756	$264,088
6	$15,585	$4,856	$20,446	$4,716	$25,156	$254,516
7	$16,246	$4,195	$20,447	$5,916	$26,356	$244,406
8	$16,767	$3,674	$20,448	$7,116	$27,556	$233,616
9	$17,127	$3,314	$20,449	$8,316	$28,756	$221,986
10	$17,347	$3,094	$20,450	$8,316	$28,756	$210,577
11	$17,466	$2,975	$20,451	$8,316	$28,756	$199,286
12	$16,468	$3,973	$20,452	$8,316	$28,756	$186,998
13	$15,382	$5,059	$20,453	$8,316	$28,756	$173,623
14	$14,199	$6,241	$20,454	$8,316	$28,756	$159,066
15	$12,913	$7,528	$20,455	$8,316	$28,756	$143,222
16	$11,512	$8,928	$20,456	$8,316	$28,756	$125,978
17	$9,988	$10,452	$20,457	$8,316	$28,756	$107,210
18	$8,329	$12,111	$20,458	$8,316	$28,756	$86,783
19	$6,524	$13,917	$20,459	$8,316	$28,756	$64,550
20	$4,558	$15,882	$20,460	$8,316	$28,756	$40,352
21	$2,420	$18,021	$20,461	$8,316	$28,756	$14,015
22	$349	$9,871	$10,242	$4,144	$14,364	$0
Totals	$281,049	$158,420	$439,722	$141,580	$581,049	

PAYING OFF A 5/1 ARM— GRADUALLY INCREASING PAYMENTS

Another scenario for John would be to bite the bullet and further take advantage of his low initial interest rate by front-loading his principal payments. If he pays $2,349—his top-rate payment—beginning with his first monthly payment, John could take a huge bite out of his loan balance when it will have the most impact. At the end of the five-year initial term, John's balance will be just $233,000. If he continues to make the same payment every month, John will save $280,000, and he'll pay off his loan in less than eighteen years.

GETTING REAL

By now, you must be thinking, *Where does this guy think I'm going to get an extra $400 or $600 a month to pay on my mortgage? I have a home loan because I don't have a lot of money, and he wants me to wave a wand and come up with extra money to add to the money I'm stretching to pay anyway.*

Maybe that's because you're spending too much of your income on house payments to begin with.

This book is about money and how to use it to achieve your dream of owning your own home—not just living in a place that you're renting from a bank, but actually owning it.

What's that worth to you? A $120-a-month cable-TV bill? A $200-a-month cell phone? One $60 tank of gasoline a month? A $10,000 Jet-Ski?

And what about your other dreams? To send your kids to a top college? To travel around the world? To open your own business? How do you plan to pay for those things if you are shelling out 30% or 40% of your income on a house for thirty or more years?

These figures are just examples, and *any* extra payment you make on your mortgage—even just $50 a month—will more than pay for itself over the long haul. Money that pays off a debt frees up future money for other purposes. That the payoff won't necessarily come for eighteen or twenty years doesn't alter that clear fact.

Anyone who has saved enough to make a substantial down payment on a home probably has acquired a savings habit already. For such people, finding an extra $400 a month is more challenge than obstacle. And the bigger question for them? Whether to pay down the mortgage or beef up the 401(k).

Even if you already own a home, you can find the money to take charge of your mortgage debt.

If you are just now looking for a home, factor in the extra payment ahead of time. Disregard what the lender says you can afford to pay, pump up the numbers in the Web "How much house can you afford?" calculator to include the extra payment, go through your own budget and find the extra money. No one, not even CEOs and movie stars, can afford to waste hundreds of thousands of dollars. That includes you.

CHAPTER 4

MAKING YOUR DEBT WORK FOR YOU

*A man builds a house in England with the expectation of
living in it and leaving it to his children; we shed our houses
in America as easily as a snail does his shell.*

— HARRIET BEECHER STOWE

There comes a time for every home owner when he needs some cash and decides the best way to get it is to borrow some of his ownership interest in his home to . . .

To do what?

It makes all the difference in the world. Borrowing that helps reduce the costs of home buying and increases your income is good, but borrowing that consumes equity and income isn't.

Refinancing your first mortgage to lower your monthly costs and your long-term interest expenses is good asset management. Taking out a second mortgage to invest in your business is tapping a cheaper money source than you could probably get with a business loan. Keeping a home-equity line of credit as a home-repair fund or even as part of your family's emergency funds can be prudent.

But be careful. Don't go wild and burden yourself with home-equity debts based on an inflated bubble-era appraisal. And whatever you do, don't use home equity to go on a spending spree, and be extra wary of lumping all your debts together under your roof.

During the heady days of the bubble, when it looked as if house prices would only keep going up, many owners used their new bricks-and-mortar wealth to buy some treats—new cars, boats, vacations. Others used their apparent gains to expand their real-estate holdings with vacation homes. Some refinanced their home loans to pay off their high-interest credit cards and other personal loans. Some doubled down on the big asset itself, remodeling the kitchen or adding a master suite.

All of these kinds of things are just what people should do with their *savings*. Treats are wonderful. Second homes are wonderful. And who doesn't dream of a new bedroom like the ones in the magazines?

But homes are not savings accounts, and these are not necessarily the smartest ways to make use of your home equity and appreciation, especially today. You never want to be in the situation of owing money on non-existent value.

Remember: The "two-fer" deal—a savings account that you live in—is a false image of home owning. A house is a hard asset, not cash, not stocks, not bonds. A house is not liquid, and it doesn't produce income. Unless you are selling and moving, the only way you can take cash out of your home is to hock it—to put it up as collateral for a loan.

And if you want to keep your home, that means you, not the house, will be paying the bills.

That's not to say that there are no times to borrow against your home. There are plenty. In this chapter, we will be looking at the use and misuse of the principal mechanisms for tapping home equity—"cash-out" refinancing of first mortgages, home-equity loans and home-equity lines of credit.

These kinds of loans give home owners real opportunities to make smart use of the money they have invested in their homes. You just want to make sure that when you're betting with that money, the house doesn't lose.

EQUITY VERSUS APPRECIATION

Although "equity" is actually any ownership interest you have in your home, I have tried to maintain a distinction throughout this book between "equity" and "appreciation."

The difference is not so important when house prices are rising. But in today's market, it might do you good to keep the two words separate in your mind, too.

Think of "equity" as the ownership interest you earn by paying down principal; "appreciation" is the ownership you win because of rising property values. Hopefully, appreciation is all that you lose in a falling market.

REFINANCING A FIRST MORTGAGE

Refinancing your primary mortgage loan is a great way to save money and improve personal monthly cash flow. But it can become a nasty money trap when you borrow your appreciation and equity, and then spend the money on things that have no investment value.

To see how equity borrowing can get out of hand, let's go back to Steve in chapter 3, the thirty-five-year-old with the fixed-rate mortgage loan.

This time we're going to change things around a bit. Let's say Steve is in a rising housing market (think 2002); his five-year-old home that he bought for $375,000 has been appreciating at a steady 7% a year; interest rates are falling. And Steve wants a boat.

Steve's not the world's best saver, but his house is. It's now worth about $525,000.

HOW TO SPOT A DUBIOUS RE-FI OFFER

Here's a list from the Federal Trade Commission of phrases and come-ons to watch out for in the advertising of mortgage refinancers:

A low "fixed" rate. Ads that tout a "fixed" rate may not tell you how long it will be "fixed." The rate may be fixed for an introductory period only, and that can be as short as thirty days.

Very low rates. Are the ads talking about a "payment" rate or the interest rate? This important detail may be buried in the fine print, if it's there at all. The interest rate is the rate used to calculate the amount of interest you will owe the lender each month. The payment rate is the rate used to calculate the amount of the payment you are obligated to make each month.

Very low payment amounts. Ads quoting a very low payment amount probably aren't telling the whole story. For example, the offer might be for an interest-only loan, where you pay only the amount of interest accrued each month. While the low payment amount may be tempting, eventually, you will have to pay off the principal.

"Mortgage rates near 30-year lows! Rates as low as 1%!" Ads with "teaser" short-term rates or payments like these don't often disclose that a rate or payment is for a very short introductory period. If you don't nail down the details in advance about your rates and payments for every month of the life of your loan, expect payment shock when the rate and payment increase dramatically.

"Important notice from your mortgage company. Open immediately." Appearances can be deceiving. Mailers that have information about your mortgage and your lender may not be from your lender at all, but rather from another company that wants your business.

"You are eligible to take part in an exclusive interest rate reduction program." Some businesses use official-looking stamps, envelopes, forms, and references to make you think their offer is from a government agency or program.

Source: Federal Trade Commission.

When he was thirty, five years ago, Steve put $75,000 down on the house and took out a $300,000, thirty-year, 6.5% fixed-rate mortgage. The loan balance is now $281,000, which means that, based on the new value of the house, Steve's equity and appreciation now equal $244,000. Not bad. It's been a real two-fer deal winner for Steve, he figures, especially since his "rent" has held steady at $1,896 a month and isn't going to go up like the ARM loan his neighbor John has.

Steve finds the boat he wants for $75,000. He also wants an extra $25,000 for a new deck and $15,000 to pay off his car and some credit cards.

He shops around for a "cash-out" refinancing deal and finds a lender who will lend him $400,000 at 5.5% on a new thirty-year loan. Transaction costs for the loan will run about $4,000, which Steve chooses to roll into the loan balance.

The best part? The new note will be just $2,271 a month. That's almost $400 more each month than Steve was paying on his old home loan, but a good deal less than the combined notes on his house, car and credit cards. And don't forget, he's getting the boat and the new deck, too. He figures it's a good deal.

But he figures wrong. Yes, Steve is lowering his monthly nut, but he's doing it by digging himself deeper and deeper into the debt hole. Buying the boat, the deck and paying off his higher interest loans with a new thirty-year mortgage will end up costing Steve an additional five years of his life and about $253,000. If he doesn't move or refinance again, Steve will be on the threshold of retirement when he finally pays off the new loan.

Put another way: Steve will spend the next thirty years paying for a boat that he's most unlikely to keep for that long, a deck that will have rotted and been replaced two or three times, a car that he'll probably trade away in a couple of years and, most insulting of all, he'll be a sixty-five-year-old grandfather paying for a dinner date that he put on his credit card when he was in his thirties. ("What *was* her name?")

Sadly, Steve's plan is not so far-fetched as it sounds. Overextended homeowners do it every day, suckered in by banks and other lenders touting the advantages of home-loan products. Even as the mortgage crisis enveloped lender after lender through 2007 and 2008, the refinancing-for-spendthrifts pitches for "good" mortgage debt went on:

- "You may be eligible to refinance your existing mortgage to a larger loan amount," Wachovia Corp. explained to mortgage shoppers in 2008. "This would provide you additional cash that could be used for debt consolidation, home improvement, or for personal use."

- "The money is yours to use any way you like—when you refinance, you can borrow additional cash to plan a dream vacation, upgrade your home, or just keep a cash reserve on hand as a financial buffer against emergencies," said the banking division of the giant Capital One Financial Corp.

- Bank of America at least added a telling footnote to its pitch: "Refinancing short-term debt may result in the payment of more interest over time, since repayment of the debt is extended."

A big problem with most "cash-out" refinancings like Steve's is that borrowers too often end up like Third World debtor countries (or the United States, for that matter). They are forever in debt to pawnbrokers—I mean bankers—using new loans to pay old loans and never getting out from under the heavier and heavier debt load.

There is a scintilla of justification for such behavior if very early in your career your income is rising rapidly and the economy is booming. But even in rising housing markets when values can clearly support additional loan burdens, it doesn't really do the up-to-their-ears-in-debt home buyers any good to keep piling on more and more borrowing. In falling or stagnant markets, home owners can end up barely hanging on to their homes, if they keep them at all.

Remember: refinancing should save you money in the long term as well as the short. Absent financial catastrophe—serious illness, prolonged disability, job loss, business failure or something else that demands you come up with a lot of cash in a hurry—a prudent home owner should never take money out of a house to use for current spending or consumer purchases. That's what savings accounts are for.

Nevertheless, there are still plenty of times when you will want to refinance and the financial conditions will be ripe.

The very best time to refinance a first mortgage is when it will enable you to both lower your monthly payment and shorten the term of the loan. Keep your first mortgage focused on paying for your house; refinance to save income, increase principal payments and cut long-term borrowing costs.

Like many modern home-owning practices, refinancing of first mortgages became popular in the inflationary 1970s and '80s. The rule of thumb for Boomer buyers was to refinance when they could get a new interest rate two percentage points lower than your old rate—10%, say, instead of 12%.

With today's lower interest rates, refinancing can pay with just one point or less difference. For example, the difference between the monthly payments on a $300,000, thirty-year loan at 7% and 6% is $1,996 versus $1,799, a sizeable savings that can be used to pay a utility bill or to fill the car with gas or, over time, to cover a year or two of college.

There are, however, other costs besides the monthly note that must be weighed. Transaction and new interest costs add up. Refinancing requires a new loan application, a new appraisal, loan points and most of the other closing costs associated with buying a house in the first place.

To calculate the actual benefit of refinancing, you must add up all the transaction costs and then divide them by the monthly payment savings. For example: If the new fees come to $3,000, and your monthly payment is $300 less, then the mortgage refinance doesn't start saving you money for ten

REFINANCING: SAVING VERSUS CASHING OUT

| Year | Original 30-year loan | | | Refinanced |
	Payments	Interest	Principal	Payments
1	$22,754	$19,401	$3,353	$22,754
2	$22,754	$19,177	$3,578	$22,754
3	$22,754	$18,937	$3,817	$22,754
4	$22,754	$18,681	$4,073	$22,754
5	$22,754	$18,409	$4,346	$22,754
Subtotal	$113,772	$94,605	$19,167	$113,772
6	$22,754	$18,118	$4,637	$20,195
7	$22,754	$17,807	$4,947	$20,195
8	$22,754	$17,476	$5,279	$20,195
9	$22,754	$17,122	$5,632	$20,195
10	$22,754	$16,745	$6,009	$20,195
11	$22,754	$16,343	$6,412	$20,195
12	$22,754	$15,913	$6,841	$20,195
13	$22,754	$15,455	$7,299	$20,195
14	$22,754	$14,966	$7,788	$20,195
15	$22,754	$14,445	$8,310	$20,195
16	$22,754	$13,888	$8,866	$20,195
17	$22,754	$13,294	$9,460	$20,195
18	$22,754	$12,661	$10,094	$20,195
19	$22,754	$11,985	$10,770	$20,195
20	$22,754	$11,263	$11,491	$20,195
21	$22,754	$10,494	$12,261	$20,195
22	$22,754	$9,673	$13,082	$20,195
23	$22,754	$8,797	$13,958	$20,195
24	$22,754	$7,862	$14,893	$20,195
25	$22,754	$6,864	$15,890	$20,195
26	$22,754	$5,800	$16,954	$20,195
27	$22,754	$4,665	$18,090	$20,195
28	$22,754	$3,453	$19,301	$20,195
29	$22,754	$2,161	$20,594	$20,195
30	$22,754	$781	$21,973	$20,195
31				
32				
33				
34				
35				
TOTAL	$682,634	$382,633	$300,000	$618,638

25-year loan		"Cash-out" refinanced loan		
Interest	Principal	Payments	Interest	Principal
$19,401	$3,353	$22,754	$19,401	$3,353
$19,177	$3,578	$22,754	$19,177	$3,578
$18,937	$3,817	$22,754	$18,937	$3,817
$18,681	$4,073	$22,754	$18,681	$4,073
$18,409	$4,346	$22,754	$18,409	$4,346
$94,605	$19,167	$113,772	$94,605	$19,167
$14,611	$5,584	$27,405	$22,066	$5,339
$14,310	$5,884	$27,405	$21,762	$5,643
$13,994	$6,201	$27,405	$21,440	$5,964
$13,660	$6,534	$27,405	$21,101	$6,304
$13,309	$6,886	$27,405	$20,742	$6,663
$12,939	$7,256	$27,405	$20,362	$7,042
$12,548	$7,646	$27,405	$19,962	$7,443
$12,137	$8,057	$27,405	$19,538	$7,867
$11,704	$8,491	$27,405	$19,090	$8,315
$11,247	$8,947	$27,405	$18,616	$8,788
$10,766	$9,429	$27,405	$18,116	$9,288
$10,259	$9,936	$27,405	$17,587	$9,817
$9,724	$10,470	$27,405	$17,028	$10,376
$9,161	$11,033	$27,405	$16,438	$10,967
$8,568	$11,627	$27,405	$15,813	$11,591
$7,943	$12,252	$27,405	$15,153	$12,251
$7,284	$12,911	$27,405	$14,456	$12,949
$6,589	$13,605	$27,405	$13,719	$13,686
$5,858	$14,337	$27,405	$12,939	$14,465
$5,087	$15,108	$27,405	$12,116	$15,289
$4,274	$15,921	$27,405	$11,245	$16,159
$3,418	$16,777	$27,405	$10,325	$17,079
$2,516	$17,679	$27,405	$9,353	$18,052
$1,565	$18,630	$27,405	$8,325	$19,079
$563	$19,632	$27,405	$7,239	$20,166
		$27,405	$6,091	$21,314
		$27,405	$4,877	$22,527
		$27,405	$3,595	$23,810
		$27,405	$2,239	$25,165
		$27,405	$806	$26,599
$318,638	**$300,000**	**$935,912**	**$516,745**	**$419,167**

months. (There's another step you can take: also figure how much more or less principal you're paying under the new loan versus what you would have paid under the old.)

When interest rates were falling rapidly in the early years of the decade, so-called "serial refinancers" negotiated new loans two or three times as rates declined from the 8% to 9% range to the 5% to 6% range. Because of the fees, many of these home buyers probably didn't see any real savings for several years.

With all that in mind, let's go back to Steve and rethink his plan.

You'll recall that he's been paying $1,896 on a 6.5%, $300,000 loan; his balance is now down to $281,000. He also knows that he can get a new thirty-year, $400,000 loan at 5.5%, plus $4,000 (1% of the loan balance) in fees.

Here's our action plan for Steve: he should forget the "cash-out" deal and concentrate, instead, on paying off his existing balance. Borrow $281,000 for twenty-five years and pay off the old balance. (Because Steve is borrowing less of the value of the house—the loan-to-value is 54% versus 76% for the cash-out loan—and for a shorter term, he can expect an even lower, 5.25%, interest rate. Steve should also pay the fees out of pocket so he won't be paying them for three decades.)

This next spreadsheet shows the results. The first three columns show the original loan and what it has cost Steve so far and what it will cost him for the next twenty-five years. The middle columns show the impact of refinancing the $281,000 balance for twenty-five years, and the far-right columns show what happens with his thirty-year, $400,000 cash-out refinancing plan.

The bottom line: Steve's refinanced loan will cost just $1,683 a month; he'll save $64,000 of long-term interest; he'll stick to his plan to be mortgage free by sixty; and he'll have an extra $213 a month to pay on his credit card and auto loans.

The cash-out deal, in contrast, extends the final mortgage payoff five more years while increasing Steve's monthly payments. And worst of all, the boat, the deck, the car loan and borrowing to pay his credit card balances will end up costing Steve more than a quarter of a million dollars! Total payments for the cash-out refinance will come to $317,000 more than if Steve refinances to a twenty-five-year loan.

You can see that Steve's smarter refinancing plan—passing on the incredibly expensive temptation to take cash out of the house with a new first mortgage and instead concentrating on paying down the loan balance—pays off in both the long term and the short. Most important, it actually gets Steve closer to his life goal of owning his home free and clear without forcing him to sacrifice his other dreams or needs.

But what about the boat? And the deck? Steve wants those, too. Shouldn't he be entitled to them?

First, no one in the world is entitled to a boat or a deck. As a human being, Steve is entitled to the necessity of a shelter. As a productive member of society, Steve can claim a degree of entitlement to the best shelter *that he can afford.*

But a boat? And a deck? If Steve wants those things and can pay for those things, then by all means he should buy them. There's no moral reason that he shouldn't borrow money to buy them, but clearly it's financially imprudent for him to take out a thirty-year loan to pay for them. Even borrowing short term—for five years, say, with a home-equity loan—would be smarter.

Steve's best, most sound, course of action, however, is to defer his purchases and apply the money he is saving on his mortgage to pay off his high interest credit cards and auto loan, and then to apply his monthly savings to his other goals.

In addition, he could take advantage of the home-building downturn and find a contractor who will build the deck cheaper; or Steve could learn to build the deck himself; or he could work out a deal with a handy friend to swap services; or he could buy the building supplies at Home Depot and hire a crew of day laborers.

Finally, the prudent Steve could hold off on the boat, save

WHY IS IT CALLED A SECOND MORTGAGE?

The difference between a first and second mortgage is where the lender stands in line to be paid. If you stop making payments, in all likelihood it will be the first-mortgage holder who will foreclose on you and sell the house.

From the proceeds of the foreclosure sale, the first dollars go to federal, state and local governments to pay any taxes that might be due.

After that come the "secured" lenders. The first-mortgage holder takes the money that's owed him (and any costs related to the foreclosure). If there's any money left, then the second-mortgage holder gets what's due him.

And so on and so on. In high-profile, multimillion-dollar foreclosures, such as those involving entertainment figures or business executives, it's not at all unusual to see mortgage holders in the third, fourth or even higher positions.

If there's still money left after all the "secured" lenders are paid, then the lien holders such as builders and remodeling contractors are paid.

Last in line is the foreclosed "owner."

his money and buy it when he can afford it. In the meantime, he can rent a boat just about any weekend at just about any marina.

Whatever Steve chooses to do, he shouldn't increase his long-term borrowing for short-term wants or needs. That's why there are other, much less expensive, ways to borrow from your biggest asset.

HOME-EQUITY LOANS AND LINES OF CREDIT

Home-equity financing, also called a "second mortgage," is a loan secured by any value of your house that exceeds the balance on the first mortgage. It's simple: if you owe $200,000 on a house appraised at $375,000, you have $175,000 equity that you may potentially be able to borrow. Even in today's tight-credit atmosphere, just about any lender will make an equity loan to a home owner with a good credit history, a house valuable enough to secure the loan and a job that pays enough to carry the added debt burden.

Second-mortgage financing works so well for home owners because it opens them to a level of relatively low-cost borrowing that would be otherwise unavailable. That's because home owners have something that most non-owners don't have—*security*.

We're not talking nuclear deterrents or personal arsenals. We're talking about the roof over your head and the floor under your children's feet, something that the lender can take away if you don't pay back the money. Inherent in all real-estate loans is a very clear, explicit threat from the lender: "If you don't repay this loan, with interest, I will have the sheriff put you and your belongings out on the street. I will take possession of the house. And I will sell it to get my money back." It may sound frightening, but having security makes it much easier to get a loan when you need it.

Non-owners usually have nothing to secure a loan but a job and a promise to pay back the money. That's why interest rates on credit card and personal loans—"unsecured" debts—are so much higher than mortgage rates. In fact, just about any type of nonbusiness loan is going to carry a higher interest rate than a loan secured by a primary residence. There are several reasons for that, but it mainly boils down to lenders assuming that distressed borrowers will make mortgage payments and try to keep their homes no matter what financial calamities befall them. (That's part of the reason so many lenders were in trouble during the credit crisis. They assumed wrong—especially when they lent money to "home owners" with no-money-down mortgages.)

The result is a pool of low-interest second-mortgage credit available to home owners to use as a substitute for high-interest unsecured *consumer* or personal credit.

LOAN-TO-VALUE RATIO

All mortgage lending, whether for first or second mortgages, is based on the value of the house and the total money borrowed against it. That's called the "loan-to-value" ratio or LTV.

Make a 20% down payment when you buy a $300,000 house and get a first mortgage for the remaining $240,000, and your loan-to-value ratio is 80%. If your house doubles in value but your mortgage balance is still about the same, your LTV is 40%. Take out a $60,000 home-equity loan to build a new kitchen, and your LTV will be 50%.

As a rule, the lower the LTV on your house, the lower your borrowing costs. That only makes sense: the less money borrowed, the more secure the loan, the lower the interest rate.

Unfortunately, during the bubble reckless lenders made loans that pushed LTVs over 100%. In other words, they made home loans that weren't secured at all by the value of the property. Protect yourself and your home: a smart home buyer should aim to have a total LTV—including the first mortgage and any other borrowing secured by the property—of no more than 80%.

Within the broad category of "home-equity financing" is a wide array of loan products. Most home owners should pay no attention to 99% of them. You need only be aware of what are generally referred to as a "home-equity loan" and a "home-equity line of credit." Both are types of second-mortgage loans, and both can be good loans to have if you use them *instead* of other higher-interest borrowing.

A home-equity loan is a traditional fixed-rate loan with a fixed term, usually from five to thirty years. You borrow the money, receive a check and then pay it back with fixed payments over the years. Interest rates can be two to three percentage points over first-mortgage rates, and interest payments on loans up to $100,000 are usually tax deductible.

A line of credit, you'll recall, is more like a credit card loan with a limit based on your total ownership interest. It features a revolving balance and an adjustable interest rate that is often quite low at first, and then resets higher in six months or a year. There's a minimum payment due every month. But like a credit card, you can choose to pay the entire balance, and you still have the credit line open for the future. In most cases, a line of credit is set up for thirty years, but you can tap the available funds for only ten or fifteen years. Then your balance is amortized over the remaining term of the loan.

Very important: borrowing against your home equity—your actual ownership interest in your home—is not the same as borrowing to buy your house. Home-equity borrowing should be viewed as short-term loans that you take out instead of *personal* or consumer debt. But don't get yourself in a situation where you are paying off home-equity loans for years and years. That will negate all the advantage you have using secured credit over unsecured because if you extend the length of the loan, the additional interest costs will more than eat up any advantage of lower interest rates you get from borrowing against your house.

That said, a short-term, fixed-rate home-equity loan can be a good alternative for handling a major personal or consumer debt such as an auto loan, education or medical expenses, starting a business or any other kind of higher-interest debt that can be paid off in just a few years. You don't want to be paying 7% or 8% interest for thirty years on a car you bought with a home-equity loan. But if you can swap a five-year, 10% auto loan with a five-year, 8% home-equity loan, then you will save a lot of money.

A short-term home-equity loan can also be used effectively to remodel the house. We'll look much more at remodeling issues in chapter 6, but for now you should be especially wary of *long-term* borrowing to pay for home improvements. If you don't have cash and need (*need,* not want) to make some improvements, then short-term borrowing is the way to go. And a

DEBT CONSOLIDATION

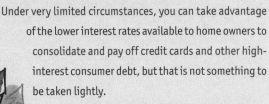

Under very limited circumstances, you can take advantage of the lower interest rates available to home owners to consolidate and pay off credit cards and other high-interest consumer debt, but that is not something to be taken lightly.

If you do need to tap your equity to get out from under onerous debt payments, it must be part of a resolute and disciplined program of permanent debt elimination. It can take decades to pay off credit cards with 20% or 25% interest rates, so a five-year home-equity loan at 7% or 8% can do wonders.

But you have to get rid of the credit cards and commit yourself to living a debt-managed life.

Never use home-equity financing merely to reduce the monthly payments or to extend the duration of consumer loans. If you have chronic problems managing your debts, then merely adding another debt to your burden will do you no good.

Soon enough, you'll be worse off than when you started. You will max out the credit cards again and be paying off your home-equity loan at the same time.

When it comes to debt consolidation, proceed with caution.

home-equity loan will be cheaper than any credit deal that the local home-improvement center offers.

As with all real-estate financing, however, home-equity loans come with large transaction costs. No matter what the lender says in its advertisements, there will be some costs; even "no fee" or "zero points" loans require some kind of appraisal and the new second mortgage has to be filed with the local government. Depending on your state, you may end up having to pay a lawyer to handle the closing and do the necessary filings. And warning: anytime new deeds or liens are filed at the

MORTGAGE ACCELERATORS

In the last few years, a new type of mortgage has appeared that combines the elements of a traditional first mortgage and a line of credit with an adjustable-interest rate and (here's the interesting part) a checking account. These "mortgage accelerator" loans are sometimes called "Australian mortgages" because they were first introduced in the United States by that country's Macquarie Bank.

What's most special about these new loans: they turn your home equity into a checking account. You deposit your paycheck into your mortgage account, and any money that is waiting to be used to pay for groceries, the kid's braces, the electric bill or any other thing you pay for out of your checking account is paying down your mortgage balance. If you spend more in a month than you make, you borrow equity. If you spend less, any money leftover pays down your balance.

It works because the first mortgage debt isn't amortized like a typical home loan with a balance computed on only the first day of every month. Rather, the Australian mortgage features revolving debt that is computed daily. So your balance fluctuates with each month's income and outflow. The more money you have in your account, the lower the daily balance. If you spend more money than your paycheck, the mortgage balance goes up.

The result? If you are disciplined and conscientious, you can pay off your mortgage very, very quickly. If you save $100 out of every paycheck or maintain a $1,500 checking account balance, then that money goes straight to paying down your mortgage. If you get a $10,000 bonus, that, too, goes straight to mortgage reduction.

When you want to spend some of your savings, however, you will end up borrowing it back from the house, just as if you tapped your line of credit. So you can see, if you don't use the account wisely, you may end up just treading water for years—borrow, pay back, borrow, pay back.

After the first ten years or so, however, the mortgage reverts to a standard amortization, so you will be forced to pay down your balance eventually.

BORROWING YOUR HOME EQUITY

	Preferred loan to value (total borrowing	What's good	What's bad
First mortgage refinance	No more than your current loan balance	Lower interest costs and monthly payments on primary mortgage	"Cash-out" refinancing increases overall mortgage debt, extends short-term borrowing, can lengthen payoff time
Home-equity loan	80% (all loans secured by the house, including first mortgage balance)	Can be used to lower interest costs, payments on short-term debts; excellent for managing higher interest borrowing	When misused to consolidate consumer debt, can result in more debt problems down the line; limited loan terms result in extra borrowing costs
Home-equity line of credit	80% (all loans, including first mortgage balance)	"Revolving" credit that can be used, paid, reused over the years; alternative to credit cards; emergency fund	Limited "draw" period; temptation to roll up large balance increasing overall debt load

courthouse, be prepared for a letter from the county assessor. You could get hit with a new, higher tax assessment based on the new value of the house.

You don't want to be forever taking out loans, paying them back and then taking out another. Nor do you want to take out a home-equity loan for a lot more than your immediate needs and then bank or invest—or worse, spend—the rest.

But all of us, home owners especially, from time to time need extra money, often exceeding the resources of even the most conscientious savers. Roofs need fixing. Furnaces die. You get the picture.

If you don't have sufficient savings to cover these kinds of things, you'll probably end up putting the bill on your credit card and paying it off over time at some outlandish interest rate.

The alternative? A home-equity line of credit, often called a "HELOC."

A line of credit operates like "revolving" credit card debt, but at a much, much lower rate of interest. Some lenders actually issue borrowers credit cards to tap the credit line; others give you checks.

Lines of credit are quite common in business, and if you approach a home line of credit with a business-like attitude, you will find a HELOC a helpful way to manage your home asset:

- Don't build up a balance and let it ride for a long time.

- Draw on the available money only when you need it.

- Pay the balance down when you can.

- Then use the money again when next you need it.

Because HELOC interest rates adjust with market conditions, you can expect that over the long haul interest rates will be higher than on traditional fixed-rate home-equity loans. But they will also be much lower than credit cards. In 2008, rates for a $50,000 HELOC (total LTV 80% or less) were in the 7% to 8% range, just half of a percentage point or so over home-equity loans but fully six or seven points below standard credit card rates.

Not a bad deal.

If you are the kind of person who regularly uses a credit card, a HELOC is a terrific mechanism for operating your property and keeping your borrowing costs in check. The lines of credit are set up like traditional home-equity loans (so there's lots of upfront paperwork with many of the same transaction costs), but you are not saddled with a large new debt. Nor do you have to go back to the lender for a new loan once this one is paid off. The revolving balance feature lets you use just what money you need when you need it and not use it when you don't.

Most lenders require an "initial draw" of some money when you open a HELOC. If you don't need that money right away, you can sit on it for a month or two or use it to pay down other debt. If you pay it back as soon as possible, you will have the open line of credit with no payments due. (Tip: paying a HELOC balance to zero may drive your lender bonkers. It might close the account. Always leave a balance of a few dollars—and remember to make the minimum payments every month—to make sure the credit line is always available.)

Finally, there is one annoying drawback to a HELOC—the "draw" versus "payback" periods. Depending on the exact terms of the loan, the revolving line of credit feature might last only five to ten years. At that point the lending aspect of the loan will stop and you will be required to pay back the balance, which will be amortized over the remaining life of the loan.

Of course, having a big new debt to pay off will not affect the smart borrower who has kept a low balance on the HELOC. But it will mean either renegotiating the terms of the HELOC or opening a new line of credit.

Less smart borrowers who have let their balance build up and then made only minimal payments will lose the borrowing flexibility altogether and face a new monthly payment.

CHAPTER 5

How to Buy a Home

The physician can bury his mistakes, but the architect can only advise his client to plant vines.

— FRANK LLOYD WRIGHT

The process of buying your first home begins long before you call up a real-estate agent or spend a Sunday afternoon visiting open houses. It begins the morning you report to your first real job or the night you realize the person you're sharing pasta with is more than just another date. Most likely, it begins the moment you realize it's time to stop living like a college student and start building a grown-up life.

In our culture, such moments of clarity inevitably focus on houses because, until now, buying a home has been Americans' ultimate settling-down experience, the essential rite of passage from frivolous youth to responsible adulthood. It has been seen as the first step of wealth building.

But should it be today?

Definitely not. Throughout this book, we've tried to separate the emotions of home owning from the economics of home buying. There's no effort here to ignore or deny the deep personal feelings and cultural attachments that Americans have about owning homes, only attempts to clarify the financial issues associated with acquiring something worth hundreds of thousands of dollars when you have to borrow the money to do it. Anyone reading this book has only so many dollars to spend on his or her needs and dreams. You will have to make choices. And the smartest choices are made with your head, not your heart.

With that in mind, this chapter will take you through some of the choices that young, early-cycle home buyers must make if and when they decide to buy a home. There's no effort here to be exhaustive, no step-by-step guide to the process of buying. There are far too many books that promise that (type "home buy" into the Amazon.com search prompt and you get more than seventeen thousand book titles). Rather, we will be looking in this chapter—and later ones—at the way you should approach the process, the thinking that can help you best reach your goals.

We'll look at the decision process that leads up to the resolution to buy, and then we'll examine some of the specific financial matters related to buying. Finally, we will zero in on the buying process itself to show you how decisions and choices made early can pay off down the road.

The smartest decisions any potential home buyer needs to ask him- or herself begin with some important questions. . . .

"WHERE DO I WANT TO BE IN TEN YEARS?"

Asking yourself this question may make you feel as if you're in a job interview, but it's a great question to help you focus on what matters to you as a potential home owner and a prudent manager of your own or your family's money.

A home is a long-term commitment, and if you don't plan to live in your house for more than a few years, you should probably not buy. In fact, that's one of the biggest home-buying mistakes most Americans make: moving too early and too often. It's a guaranteed money eater.

That's because the transaction costs associated with buying

and selling a home are outrageous. Loan points. Appraisals. Lawyers. Private mortgage insurance. Inspections. Document fees. Conveyance fees. Aargh!

You aren't likely to get into or out of a house without paying a great deal of money for the privilege of "owning" it—3% to 5% of the price when you are buying, plus "I-have-to-pay-something" costs for the years you're in the place, and then 6% to 8% when you sell.

On top of all that, if you stay in a house for just a few years, you won't make much of a dent in the mortgage principal. And, as we have already seen, you won't be able to count on a rising housing market to help you out either.

Let's look at some numbers. Here's a spreadsheet on a moderately priced home theoretically bought in bubble-era 2006 and sold in 2016. You can see that even with substantial price appreciation—something you can't plan on for the next few years—the owner of this house will be hard-pressed to make any sort of profit.

In the short term, there's just no getting around most home-buying costs. Mortgages will always load interest at the front, and there will always be third, fourth and fifth parties standing in line to take their pieces out of real-estate transactions. Rising housing markets sometimes can compensate, but falling or stagnant prices won't.

When you're in an older house in an existing neighborhood, you will have fix-up costs and, quite likely, some major repairs. Buy a new place in a developing area, and your maintenance costs will be low, but commuting costs will be considerable—and when it's time to sell, you'll be competing for buyers with new-home builders offering more up-to-date places nearby.

The best way to deal with home-buying costs is to minimize them when you have to pay them, and stay in one place long enough to amortize them over a long period of time. It's great if you talk the lender down to just $300 on the appraisal fee. It's even better if you have to pay for an appraisal only once or twice in your lifetime.

OWNING A HOME FOR 10 YEARS

2006 purchase price			$290,000		
Annual price change	7%	3%	0%	−1%	−3%
2016 sale price	**$570,000**	**$390,000**	**$290,000**	**$262,000**	**$214,000**
Mortgage loan balance	$197,000	$197,000	$197,000	$197,000	$197,000
Sales commission and move-out costs (8% of sale price)	$45,600	$31,200	$23,200	$20,960	$17,120
Gross sale proceeds	**$327,400**	**$161,800**	**$69,800**	**$44,040**	**($120)**
Down payment (20%)	$58,000	$58,000	$58,000	$58,000	$58,000
Principal payments	$35,000	$35,000	$35,000	$35,000	$35,000
Net sale proceeds	**$234,400**	**$68,800**	**($23,200)**	**($48,960)**	**($93,120)**
Borrowing costs					
Mortgage interest (before income tax)	$141,000	$141,000	$141,000	$141,000	$141,000
Operating expenses ("I-have-to-pay something" costs)					
Transaction and move-in costs (3% of purchase price)	$8,700	$8,700	$8,700	$8,700	$8,700
Property taxes ($5,000/year, before income tax)	$50,000	$50,000	$50,000	$50,000	$50,000
Insurance ($1,000/year)	$10,000	$10,000	$10,000	$10,000	$10,000
Maintenance, minor repairs, community fees ($300/month)	$36,000	$36,000	$36,000	$36,000	$36,000
Minor renovations (exterior and interior paint, carpets)	$15,000	$15,000	$15,000	$15,000	$15,000
Total operating costs	$119,700	$119,700	$119,700	$119,700	$119,700
Profit / (loss)	**($26,300)**	**($191,900)**	**($283,900)**	**($309,660)**	**($353,820)**

"IS BUYING A HOME THE BEST USE OF MY MONEY?"

This question is typically framed for most potential home buyers as, "Is it better for me to rent or buy?" But that's really only part of what you should be considering. As important as the rent-or-buy decision is, figuring out where buying a home fits in with your other financial obligations and goals is much more vital.

Because more loans are used to fund higher education today (rather than grants), most young people are starting their adult lives deeper in the hole than their parents or grandparents did. Add to that the decline of traditional pension plans and uncertainty about the future of Social Security and Medicare, and young adults in their twenties and early thirties have much graver financial concerns than whether they should rent or buy a house.

Only after you have your student loans under control and have a long-term retirement-savings plan in place should you turn your attention toward a home. Not dealing with those issues first—buying a house and adding thirty years of mortgage payments on top of your other obligations—will only increase, not alleviate, your anxieties and money problems.

Beyond the issues of school debt and long-term savings, however, another fundamental issue is what kind of return on your investment does a house promise? Think like a property investor, not a potential home owner, for a moment and project out a few years. Will you be ahead if you buy? Or should you stay where you are, keep renting and invest instead?

Doug Guillaume, a chemical salesman in Houston, learned the answer the hard way, only *after* he had been a home buyer for a while.

After Doug sold his house in suburban New Orleans for $225,000 in October 2006, to transfer to Houston, he did some math. He wanted to find out two things: How had his investment in real estate performed? And should he buy a new house? He knew the answer to question No. 1 would direct him to the right answer to question No. 2.

He was surprised by the outcome. "When I added up all my expenses for repairs, insurance, property taxes, interest, closing costs to buy and sell, real-estate agent commissions, title fees, title insurance and interest-tax deductions, etc. etc. etc.," he says, "I realized I had barely made 5% on my money."

Doug, who is single, bought the house in December 2000, when he was twenty-five years old. He paid $142,000, putting about $5,000 down and financing the rest with a thirty-year, 5.75% loan. Five years later, in January 2006, he had paid off his mortgage.

"It was very disturbing," he says, to realize just how expensive his foray into home owning actually had been. Yes, he had made a modest profit, but not enough to justify the time and hard work of owning his own home. "What I came to was it's not an investment. It's just something you buy because you like it.

"If you like owning a home, go ahead and do it. If you think it's an investment, and you don't enjoy the house, then it's not worth it."

When Doug sold, after paying his commission and other closing and moving costs, his "rebate" came to $215,000, which he invested in U.S. Treasury bonds. He's now renting in Houston.

"When I discuss this with my friends, they all look at me like I was the first person to tell them that Santa Claus doesn't exist," he says. "So, I don't discuss this anymore."

In a healthy, rising market such as the United States knew for most of the last sixty years, a story like Doug's was practically unthinkable. It was the most conventional wisdom that a home buyer would do better financially than a renter over the long term. But that's hardly a sure thing in the current climate, certainly if your idea of the long term falls somewhere short of twenty years. If house prices in your area are stagnant or rising only moderately, the renter who invests the equivalent of a down payment can do far better than a buyer over a considerable time.

In 2007, my colleague Jack Hough, who evaluates stocks for *SmartMoney* magazine, wrote a thoughtful and provocative article for the magazine's Web site comparing the long-term, after-inflation investment returns of houses to stocks.

He treated renting and buying from the point of view of an investor, examining the relationship between corporate

	BEST USE OF MY MONEY? RENTING VERSUS BUYING				
Month	John's monthly payment	John's payment after tax savings	Steve's monthly rent	Steve's investment value	John's home equity
1	$8,102	$6,228	$5,000	$267,636	$144,552
13	$8,167	$6,306	$5,150	$301,609	$187,627
25	$8,234	$6,387	$5,305	$337,072	$232,384
37	$8,303	$6,471	$5,464	$374,111	$278,901
49	$8,374	$6,558	$5,628	$412,819	$327,258
61	$8,447	$6,649	$5,796	$453,295	$377,540
73	$8,522	$6,743	$5,970	$495,645	$429,837
85	$8,599	$6,841	$6,149	$539,984	$484,243
97	$8,679	$6,944	$6,334	$586,434	$540,857
121	$8,846	$7,161	$6,720	$686,198	$661,135
133	$8,933	$7,276	$6,921	$739,805	$725,027
145	$9,022	$7,396	$7,129	$796,108	$791,582
146	$9,022	$7,399	$7,129	$800,879	$797,295
147	$9,022	$7,402	$7,129	$805,681	$803,018
148	$9,022	$7,406	$7,129	$810,514	$808,751
149	$9,022	$7,409	$7,129	$815,377	$814,494
150	**$9,022**	**$7,412**	**$7,129**	**$820,271**	**$820,248**
151	$9,022	$7,416	$7,129	$825,196	$826,012
152	$9,022	$7,419	$7,129	$830,152	$831,786
153	$9,022	$7,423	$7,129	$835,140	$837,571

earnings (profits) and share prices and real-estate earnings (rents) and home prices. It was an eye-opener for many of his readers.

"Over the next twenty years," he wrote, "I believe houses will return zero or slightly less after inflation, and that stocks will return 7%."

With that sobering prediction in mind, let's revisit neighbors Steve and John. Each has now sold the house he had in chapter 3, walking away with $265,000. And they have decided,

Month	John's monthly payment	John's payment after tax savings	Steve's monthly rent	Steve's investment value	John's home equity
154	$9,022	$7,426	$7,129	$840,159	$843,366
155	$9,022	$7,430	$7,129	$845,210	$849,172
156	$9,022	$7,433	$7,129	$850,293	$854,988
157	$9,115	$7,521	$7,343	$855,279	$860,930
169	$9,210	$7,651	$7,563	$917,507	$933,210
181	**$9,308**	**$7,787**	**$7,790**	**$982,992**	**$1,008,564**
193	$9,409	$7,928	$8,024	$1,051,949	$1,087,148
205	$9,513	$8,076	$8,264	$1,124,611	$1,169,121
217	$9,620	$8,230	$8,512	$1,201,227	$1,254,656
349	$11,034	$10,454	$11,783	$2,398,212	$2,490,536
350	$11,034	$10,464	$11,783	$2,410,453	$2,502,503
351	$11,034	$10,474	$11,783	$2,422,773	$2,514,501
352	$11,034	$10,484	$11,783	$2,435,172	$2,526,529
353	$11,034	$10,494	$11,783	$2,447,653	$2,538,588
354	$11,034	$10,504	$11,783	$2,460,213	$2,550,677
355	$11,034	$10,514	$11,783	$2,472,855	$2,562,798
356	$11,034	$10,525	$11,783	$2,485,579	$2,574,950
357	$11,034	$10,535	$11,783	$2,498,385	$2,587,133
358	$11,034	$10,545	$11,783	$2,511,274	$2,599,347
359	$11,034	$10,556	$11,783	$2,524,246	$2,611,594
360	**$11,034**	**$10,566**	**$11,783**	**$2,537,302**	**$2,623,871**

like the Jeffersons in the 1970s TV sitcom, to move up to a "deluxe apartment"—identical 1,400-square-foot, three-bedroom, two-bath co-ops—on Manhattan's Upper East Side. (These numbers may seem outlandish to many readers outside New York City, but, trust me, they are quite typical. Indeed, the purchase prices are on the low side for the 2007–2008 market.)

John took advantage of the softening real-estate market and paid $1,175,000 for an apartment that was priced at $1,395,000, which is good because it cost him $30,000 in transaction costs to buy the place. In the first year, his new home cost him $8,100 a month, including $5,940 on his loan, plus another $2,015 for insurance, taxes and "maintenance" to cover the building's mortgage, staff and upkeep. He expects 3% annual appreciation, keeping even with inflation. The calculations in the preceding table are from a dinkeytown.net calculator.

Steve decided, however, to invest his sale proceeds in a broad-market index fund that historically grows at about 7% a year and to rent his new place for $5,000 a month. He's also decided to continue investing the difference between his rent and John's monthly costs.

Who's putting his money to the best use? Believe it or not, on a net-worth basis over a very long period of time, it's pretty much a wash on paper. John's home equity won't match Steve's investment for nearly thirteen years (150 months), and it will be fifteen years before John's monthly after-tax home-buying costs are less than Steve's monthly rent.

In the long term, thirty years, the neighbors will come out with virtually the same levels of pre-tax wealth. When John cashes out and sells his condo, he will end up paying about $175,000 to Uncle Sam. It's difficult to imagine why Steve would need to cash out his investment portfolio, but if he did, he'd have a tax bill of about $340,000. Because both live in high-tax New York, their ultimate tax bills will be higher.

As you can see, absent a huge spike in real-estate prices such as during the bubble, it's only the tax laws that make John's home buying appear better than Steve's renting and stock investing.

There is one other big difference, however, between the neighbors' situations—"liquidity." When investors use that term, they are describing how fast something can be converted to cash. Even in a hot market, real estate is famously illiquid because it takes months to sell a property or just to borrow against it.

No one would be surprised if it took John three to six months between the time he decides to sell and the day he finally gets his check and moves out. (Or a couple of months to apply for a new "cash-out" refinanced mortgage or line of credit.) Renter Steve, on the other hand, could decide in the morning to sell just a portion of his stock online and be toasting his success in Palm Beach that evening.

And unlike John, who sold his home to reap his windfall, Steve would still have his (rented) home to come home to.

"WILL BUYING A HOME MAKE MY LIFE BETTER?"

Buying a house isn't going to solve any of your life problems. It won't repair a broken marriage, and it won't straighten out a troubled teenager. Buying a house won't make you thinner, nor does it mean you're smarter. And as millions of Americans are learning, buying a house won't even make you richer.

The arguments for buying a home inevitably come down to a collection of social positives that have been widely accepted by Americans and their leaders. Indeed, home owning is right up there with family values, cheap gasoline and a global military presence when it comes to issues that are off the debating agenda of U.S. politicians, Sunday-morning TV commentators and the public.

"A nation of home owners, of people who own a real share in their own land, is unconquerable," wrote President Franklin Roosevelt to a World War II–era meeting of savings and loan executives.

More than half a century later, President George W. Bush said: "Homeownership is a key to upward mobility for low- and middle-income Americans. It is an anchor for families and a source of stability for communities."

Undeniably, buying a house can make you feel very, very good, especially if you really can afford to buy and you do it at a time in your life when you are doing well financially and you are ready to settle down. Of course, owning a home isn't required for that kind of life, but that kind of life makes owning a home more practical.

Financial problems arise, however, for far too many home buyers who equate owning a home with living life well. They don't always go together.

Remember: a home is a reward for, not the means to, a well-managed life.

Consider the case of the Montes family in Fullerton, California. Mario and Leticia, who have two teenage daughters, were caught in the credit crunch of 2007. With a combined salary of just $90,000, the couple bought a house in 2005 for $567,000 in one of the hottest, most expensive markets in the country, Orange County, California. They put nothing down and took out two loans—one to cover about 80% of the home price and the other, a "piggyback" loan, for the rest.

The family moved into their stucco bungalow with a hot tub and hung a sign on the front door reading, "Life is a daily celebration of love." Within months, though, my *Wall Street Journal* colleagues James R. Hagerty and Ken Gepfert were reporting on the big increase in taxes and increased monthly payments that the family faced.

"Whoa!" was Mario's reaction. "I can't afford this. I went into emergency mode."

Less than two years later, the Montes family was girding for another increase that would boost monthly costs to more than half their incomes. Mario had taken on a second job and was contemplating a third. And, still, the family was facing foreclosure and losing their house.

For the Montes family, this was the tarnished reward for being hardworking, good people who didn't understand the problems they faced buying a home they couldn't afford. All they did was what the culture tells them to do: buy a house.

The cautionary lesson in their story? Home-buying problems, like any money problems, can pose strains and threats to your family life and well-being. No stucco bungalow should be so important that it's worth working three jobs just to pay for it, and the "pride of ownership" isn't worth fretting over whether you can afford to send your daughters to college.

For a home buyer, the question boils down to whether you and your lifestyle can handle the additional strains that come with buying a house. If not, then don't buy, or move to a less expensive market.

But if you think you can handle the additional problems, keep reading.

THINK LIKE AN INVESTOR

There's an old saw among real-estate investors: "I make my money on a building the day I buy it." It's a lesson that home buyers should take to heart.

No one ever made a fortune in real estate by falling in love with a property, and then paying the asking price. But that's pretty much how most home buyers end up acquiring their biggest assets. They look around at a few places, find a house they like, see what other houses in the neighborhood sold for, make an offer and then borrow hundreds of thousands of dollars to buy it.

Yes, buyers may quibble on the margins—offering a few thousand less, knowing sellers always have a number they'll take versus what they ask, or maybe insisting that the price include kitchen appliances along with the living room drapes. But the nitty gritty of negotiating a proper price based on what the property is actually worth rarely even enters the discussion.

That's because home buying is a retail business, where neither buyers nor sellers have a clue about what a house is actually worth. Everyone thinks *price* equals *value*.

The most basic metrics of home valuation are the "comps" or "comparable sale prices" that real-estate agents use to show the price of a house vis-à-vis other nearby properties. Comps are valuable, but only to a point. They give you no better picture of the actual investment value of a house than today's ticker price tells you the value of a stock.

In other words, both tell you what people are paying, but not the intrinsic value of the investment itself. For that you need to know the house's capacity to produce income. For a stock, a company or an office building—and for any real *investment*—the value isn't determined by the price, but rather by the relationship between the price of the investment and what it earns or has the potential to earn.

With bonds, that's called the "yield," or interest, as a percentage of the purchase price. A high-yield, high-risk bond in today's market might pay its owner 11% or 12% a year, whereas no-risk U.S. government bonds pay less than 5%.

In stocks, the relationship between price and profits is expressed as a "price-earnings ratio" or P/E. A solid, well-established company will have a relatively low P/E (expressed as, for example, 10/1 or just 10), reflecting its capacity to produce current income but not necessarily a lot of growth. A hot, up-and-coming growth stock, on the other hand, may have a very high P/E (60/1 or 60), reflecting stock buyers' belief in the company's ability to produce greater earnings in the future.

For example, FTD Group, the florists, has a P/E of about only 8 with a hefty annual dividend. Google is 46, and it pays no dividend. Amateur home buyers (and most of us are amateurs) tend to treat houses like Google, forever betting on the big payoff in the future. Real-estate investors, on the other hand, are usually shopping for the equivalent of FTD. During the bubble era, one of the clearest signs of the housing market's coming troubles was the rush of new home buyers and new property speculators bidding up the costs of houses. They even made TV shows about them.

Those buyers were looking to make real profits with their homes, but they were learning the wrong lessons from the home-owning industry. Remember: Houses don't make money. They cost money.

Back to the stock analogy: A company's value increases

(and its stock price goes up) when management rolls out new products or cuts costs to increase profits. Apartment buildings increase in value when landlords improve individual apartments and raise rents or install pay laundry rooms, wireless Internet access or other revenue enhancements. Even the owner of your corner coffeehouse makes her business more valuable when she buys a new espresso machine and charges $4 for each cup she makes with it.

But a house just *sits* there. Yes, some owners make improvements in their homes but, as you will see in chapter 6, few of those even make back the money the owner spent. No, home owners actually do, or can do, very little to increase the value of their properties. They must rely, instead, on a rising tide of prices that lifts the prices of all homes. Every now and then the tide rushes in and raises prices 10%, 15%, 20% a year for a few years. And every now and then, the tide rushes out again.

Successful investors will buy at low tide and sell at high. Professional investors who bought distressed properties in the down market of the early 1990s found prices in the early 2000s far too high to justify further investments. So they sold out . . . to the amateurs.

Today and for the foreseeable future, housing prices are in general decline. House prices will find their level, and it is certain to be well below where they were in the first five years of the new century. Not all markets will see the same price decline; the hottest bubble-era markets will see the biggest price ebbs while cities that didn't see big price run-ups may see only modest falloffs or even some price increases.

Some houses in some areas have already been priced 30% or 40% below their bubble-era values—those are bargains right now and could turn out to be good investments for new buyers. Others haven't found their new, lower level yet, because some hopeful sellers still believe that they will somehow withstand the outgoing tide. They won't. Eventually, if they must sell, they will capitulate and sell at the market price. Your job as a smart buyer is to be there when they do.

DETERMINING VALUE

Of course, single-family, owner-occupied homes are not in-come-producing properties, so the analogy of home buying to real-estate investing or stock investing isn't perfect, but it is, nonetheless, perfectly useful.

Even in a family home, investment metrics are enlightening. The price the buyer pays (as opposed to the price the seller asks) should be based on something more substantial than just what a similar house three blocks away sold for two months ago. Homes are not, after all, rare Renaissance paintings or precious antiques. They're mass-produced goods. Hundreds of thousands of new ones are built every year. Millions of existing homes go on the market every year.

Most amateur buyers of single-family homes end up paying more than they should because the only pricing information that real-estate agents and amateur home sellers seem to deal with are comps. If you want to find out more, you'll have to do some work on your own.

There are two other ways besides comparable sales: the rental value of the house and the replacement value. Both are used by professional appraisers along with sales comps, but rental value is the easier to estimate and most useful when buying an existing home. You can find it just reading newspaper ads or online postings at Craigslist.com. Look for what rents landlords charge for similar properties nearby.

The best question a buyer can ask a seller is, "What would this house rent for?" From there, it's a simple bit of arithmetic to determine the investment quality of a property—that is determining whether the house could pay for itself if you bought it and rented it out rather than live in it yourself. There's your value: Does the rental income cover all the costs of owning the house?

Let's take Realtor.com to Beverly Hills, site of some of the most expensive homes in the country. We'll go in the "flats," zip code 90212, where someone who hasn't had a hit feature film *might* find an affordable place to live. There it is: the cheapest two-bedroom, two-bath condo in town. Asking price: $539,000. Estimated payment (with 20% down, $106,000): $2,700 a month; common charges: $600 a month; property taxes $600. Total monthly costs: $3,900.

One block away, in a very similar building is a two-bedroom, two-bath rental apartment. The landlord is asking $2,750.

So, is the condo—the cheapest place in one of the most expensive towns in the country—a good deal? This is not a simple rent versus buy calculation. Rather, we're looking at the condo's *investment* potential in order to better gauge its value.

A typical home buyer's thinking would go something like, "What a bargain! The after-tax cost of owning is virtually the same as renting. And this place will be worth $1 million in ten years."

But here's what a property investor sees: "At this price the place loses $1,150 a month—that's $13,000 a year! It's not worth more than $300,000 . . . $350,000 max. That's what the rent can cover."

So are these people really looking at the same property? Yes, and the home buyer can learn a lot from the investor. Think like a professional: buy cheaper, or don't buy at all.

Unless he's acquiring a foreclosure or some other distressed property, a real-estate investor rarely buys a house or a small building for its hoped-for appreciated value at some indeterminate time in the future. He buys current "cash flow" and tax deductions. At a $350,000 purchase price, for example, this condo would cost the investor about $2,300 a month to operate while producing about $450 a month in positive cash flow. That's $5,400 a year, a respectable 7.7% dividend on his $70,000 down payment. The investor also gets a whopping $12,700 a year of depreciation that he will use for income-tax purposes to reduce other income dollar-for-dollar and cut his taxes. (The condo is not an investor's buy at the full asking price of $539,000. There would be $19,600 in depreciation write-offs each year, but the negative cash flow of $13,000 would negate most of the tax benefits.)

Although an investor may factor in some opportunity for price appreciation—especially if he's getting a great deal on a home in a good neighborhood or a unit in a desirable condominium development—such opportunities will appeal to an investor only if he can count on flipping the house or condo very quickly. (As anyone who has watched any of the home-flipping cable-TV shows knows, the formula is: "Buy it. Clean it. Fix it. Paint it. Sell it." In thirty minutes.)

A real-estate investor understands that, like FTD, the real value of a property to be held long term is determined by its current and potential income production—its capacity to pay all of its costs through rents and to produce a profit. An investor calculates the purchase price of a property based on its income, operating expenses, borrowing costs and the overall return when compared to alternative investments. If the numbers don't add up in the investor's favor, no amount of dreaming or hoping for a price rise will make it an economical investment.

Most home buyers, on the other hand, operate like speculators. Like stock investors betting that Google can only go up, home-buying speculators are expecting that appreciation will save them from their financial miscalculations and that they will be able to raise the price of the property when it comes time to sell. Such a home buyer has an additional burden in that selling a home must not only put money in the bank, but it also has to make enough profit to buy a new home.

(Let's indulge, for a moment, the typical home owner's mistaken belief that "imputed rent"—money a home owner doesn't spend renting—somehow compensates for the expense of buying. We know the rental income. Even allowing the $2,750 a month for imputed rent, this property would still be running a $13,000 a year negative cash flow, so the buyer is still "not paying" enough imputed rent to make a profit.)

What *can* a home buyer do to make more prudent deals?

Of course, no house seller is going to knock off 40% of his asking price just because you wave a copy of this book in front of him. The seller doesn't care if his property isn't priced to benefit you. He's expecting a greater fool to walk in the door. In a hot market, a buyer's wisest, best move may very well be just to not buy. Rent for $2,750 and save $13,000 a year. Prices will settle down soon enough. That's when the buyers—and fools—aren't so abundant. That's today's housing market, and buyers again have the upper hand in house deals.

DON'T BE FOOLED AGAIN

In much of the country—especially in the once hot bubble markets on the coasts, in the Southwest, in Florida and in major metropolitan areas—there are once-in-a-lifetime opportunities to make great deals buying homes. There's an abundance of supply and relatively limited demand. The national economy is dicey. And there's a fierce grip on the amount of mortgage money available to borrow. What an opportunity for home buyers!

The goal of any smart buyer today should be to acquire a home for well below—in many places 30% to 40% below—the property's bubble-era 2005–2007 value. Be tough, and you could find some properties at less than half their bubble-era values.

There are tens of thousands of bank-owned properties that lenders need to dump. There are distressed properties that are on the verge of foreclosure. There are home owners who have lost jobs or are relocating and have to sell as soon as possible. Anyone with some cash, good credit and a secure job who wants to buy a house should have little problem in these market conditions.

You will need to act when you do find your great home-buying value. In the meantime, here's what you need to do to get ready:

Get your finances in order. The more money you have on hand and the better your credit rating, the better your position when you go shopping. As we've noted earlier, you shouldn't even entertain the idea of buying a house until your debts are under control, you are paying into your retirement plan and you have saved a 20% down payment.

You will also need to check your credit rating and fix any problems there. Especially in this tight-lending environment, the better your credit report, the easier it will be to get a loan and the lower the interest rate.

If you need more motivation, think of it this way: good credit makes a huge difference in what a house will cost you. Fair Issac Corp. (the company that assigns FICO credit scores) has an enlightening Web page that clearly shows how valuable a credit rating is to a home buyer *(http://www.myfico.com/myfico/ CreditCentral/LoanRates.asp)*. In early 2008, the mortgage interest rate spread between a top FICO scoring borrower (above 720) and a low scorer (below 560) was more than seven percentage points! Translated into payments on a $300,000 loan, the high scorer would pay $1,724 a month ($362,000 in total interest over thirty years) versus the low scorer paying $3,314 a month and a frightening $893,000 interest over the life of the loan. Even a middling scorer can end up paying $300 a month more than someone with a high FICO number.

Also, if you are borrowing some of your down payment from parents or other relatives, you'll want to deposit the money in your savings account and let it sit for at least four months before you apply for a loan.

Get to know your banker. One of the biggest errors made by novice home buyers is finding a house before they find the money to buy it. If you want to make the best deal you can on a house, get as much of the loan process as possible out of the way before you start looking at properties.

Here's the paper you'll need at a minimum (go ahead and start gathering):

CHECKING AND CLEARING YOUR CREDIT RATING

Checking your credit reports is not difficult. Anyone is entitled to a free copy of his or her credit reports once a year from each of the Big Three credit-reporting companies. Fill out your information at *https://www.annualcredit report.com* (note the "s" in https; that means it's a secure site) or contact each of the credit agencies individually:

Equifax
P.O. Box 105873
Atlanta, GA 30348
(800) 685-1111
http://www.equifax.com

Experian
P.O. Box 2104
Allen, TX 75013
1-(888) 397-3742
http://www.experian.com

Trans Union LLC
P.O. Box 390
Springfield, PA 19064
(800) 888-4213
http://www.transunion.com

You can also write to get the three reports:

Annual Credit Report Request Service
P.O. Box 105281
Atlanta, GA 30348-5281

Be aware that your credit reports don't include your credit score. You have to pay about $8 to see your FICO score itself. You can make the request at the same time you are asking for your reports.

You can dispute anything that's wrong in your reports, but it's the ac-curate stuff that can kill you. Clearing up your credit takes a long time. Records on credit cards, for instance, go back four years or more. Some reports go back a decade. Generally, on-time payments made over the last couple of years will undo, or at least mitigate, a lot of problems from before. You may not hit the top FICO score, but you will be on the upper end of things, and a sympathetic banker might see that you have taken control of your credit and handled your debts responsibly.

Best plan from the beginning? Don't get behind in the first place, and don't let your credit run away from you. Pay your bills on time, keep your credit cards well below their limits and pay off some biggies such as auto loans or other installment purchases.

If you do find mistakes on your credit report, you can write the credit companies from the Web site where you view your report.

- A proper financial statement showing all your liquid assets (savings, checking, brokerage accounts, 401(k) balance), your debts (college, auto, credit cards) and, subtracting the latter from the former, your net worth. It's a simple, one-page layout: assets, liabilities, net worth.

- Two years of federal tax returns.

- Three months of bank statements that show the down payment money is in your account.

- Up to four recent paycheck stubs.

- A letter from your boss or company confirming your employment.

- A "gift" letter, if your parents or others are giving you the money for the down payment. The letter should state that the down payment is a gift, not a loan, and that you are not obligated to pay the money back.

If you are a first-time buyer, you need to visit prospective lenders in person, not online, not on the phone. Try to avoid

THREE IMPORTANT QUESTIONS TO ASK A LENDER

1. **"What's your housing-to-income ratio?"** Banks can differ on this, but the general rule of thumb is 28% of your monthly gross income going to your mortgage and other monthly housing expenses. Lenders are much firmer on this today than they were in the bubble era. In high-cost areas, lenders would allow ratios well over 40%. Readers of this book should be aiming for 25% or less.

2. **"What's your income-to-debt ratio?"** Today, the ceiling for all your other debts—autos, credit cards, school—is no more than 36%. That is an additional 8% of your income going to debt repayments over your monthly housing costs. Although you may not have your school loans paid off, you should have no consumer loans outstanding when you go house shopping.

3. **"Do you hold and service your own loans?"** Lenders that keep "portfolio loans" on their own books rather than selling them to Fannie Mae, Freddie Mac or the open market have far greater lending flexibility. That will be especially helpful to you if you are buying a distressed property or if you have credit or income problems in your past. Likewise, some lenders farm out the day-to-day job of managing borrowers' accounts to sending statements and keeping up with payments to third parties. You'd prefer dealing with a lender that handles its own paperwork.

For a more complete rundown of questions, see "20 Questions to Ask a Lender or Mortgage Broker," a pamphlet by the California Department of Corporations. It's available online at: *http://www.corp.ca.gov/Education_Outreach/pdf/resources/mort20quest.pdf*.

mortgage brokers and deal directly with lenders. I recommend first going to small lenders, a credit union or a local bank, preferably in the neighborhood or town where you are looking to buy. Although there's nothing inherently wrong with brokers, big banks or online lending sites—they'll have a wide selection of loan products to show you. You might prefer more personal service both before and after you get the loan than you can expect from those big lenders. Especially since you're organized, liquid, ready to get going and interested in only straightforward fixed-rate loans or simple ARMs.

Plus, credit unions and smaller banks, including not-so-small regional banks, are more likely to hold and service their own loans rather than sell them in the secondary mortgage market like big lenders do. Smaller lenders are also likely to be much more attuned to individuals and local conditions. When you're sitting across a desk from the bank's loan officer, it gives him or her an opportunity to judge you personally as opposed to just a set of numbers entered into a programmed lending algorithm.

Besides, you want to build a relationship that's going to last a long, long time (maybe you'll invite your loan officer to *your* mortgage burning), and the best way to do that is to know the people at the bank and for them to know you.

Although we're talking about starting the loan process before you're ready to buy, you should know that no bank, large or small, is going to OK a loan before you have a place picked out and a contract signed. But getting a pre-approval from the person who is now your *personal* banker will give you a powerful negotiating tool when it comes to making an offer on a house. (Go ahead, put his office number on your cell phone speed dial.)

Why? Pre-approval means you can close the deal quicker. During the bubble, sellers might have required pre-qualifications or pre-approvals just to weed out the serious buyers from the looky-loos. But today, having your banker behind you when you walk in the front door puts the weight of performance on the seller. It won't be a matter of you, the buyer, qualifying to buy the house. Rather, it will be whether the seller's house qualifies for you.

Once you have your figure—what the bank will lend you and what you are willing to pay—it's time to go shopping.

SPACE. PRICE. LOCATION.

Here's a rule of thumb to keep in mind as you shop for a new home. Because most home buyers have limited resources, we all have to make trade-offs. Keep your perspective: you can get a new home for the price you want or you can get the space you want or you can get the location you want. But you can't have all three.

If you want the biggest, fanciest house in the very best part of town, the price will be the size of a small nation's annual budget. If you don't have that kind of money but want to stay in the silk stocking district, you will have to buy a much more modest home.

If you are willing to commute for two hours or can handle some of the more rugged parts of town, you can find a really big house at a good price.

Space. Price. Location. Pick two.

Decide what you want. Do you need three bedrooms and two baths? Do you want a family room and a living room? A large backyard or access to a park? A two-car garage or good public transportation? Make a list of the physical elements of a house that you need and those you want. Decide what you have to have now and what can be added later. Be complete, be honest and be ruthless.

Make yourself a "shopping list" that includes everything you wrote down and keep it handy when you start looking for a place. And like a smart shopper at the supermarket, be resolute. Don't let yourself be swayed by items you aren't shopping for. Yes, it *would* be nice to have a breakfast nook. But $20,000-over-budget nice?

Learn about the market. Next, educate yourself about neighborhoods.

The old broker's cliché—the three most important things about real estate are location, location, location—is true. Nothing beats a good neighborhood with a good school when it comes to buying a home. The best deal you can make ever is to buy the cheapest property in the best part of town.

That said, you must also be realistic. If you can't afford a $539,000 place to live, you can't afford it just as much in Beverly Hills as anywhere else. If you must live in Beverly Hills, you should be prepared to pay for it today and for a long, long time.

The better alternative is to be flexible and find out where people like you are moving. Ask around at the office or church. Look. There's a good chance there's a healthy, relatively inexpensive alternative neighborhood that will suit you and your family just great.

You can tell what neighborhood works best for you just by walking around. Don't rely on real-estate agents to be your tour guides, though. A good real-estate agent can make any neighborhood sound like it's for you.

Instead, get to know the place. Seek out locals at neighborhood stores or restaurants. Check out schools and crime statistics yourself with the local government. Many school districts and police departments keep basic statistical information available online. The local newspaper will have information, too.

Many older cities and suburbs have "mixed-use" neighborhoods that feature pedestrian-friendly commercial areas along with modest houses and apartment buildings. You might even find an aging factory that has been converted to trendy offices, shops or condominiums. In some older downtowns, you will see early twentieth-century high-rise office buildings converted to apartments with the lower floors given over to restaurants and chic retailers.

Newer cities and suburbs are more segregated by use and more automobile dependent with their distinct commercial

WHAT A BUYER NEEDS TO KNOW ABOUT REAL-ESTATE AGENTS

There's absolutely nothing wrong with real-estate agents. A good, attentive agent performs valuable services for both sellers and buyers.

Not only do agents handle the nuts and bolts of selling a property, but they help both sellers and buyers through the difficult, trying buying process. Most people don't have much experience buying homes, but good agents are experts on it, closing deals all the time, twice a month or more during busy seasons. Top-producing agents in busy areas can close scores of transactions a year.

But the main thing that most buyers need to know about a typical real-estate agent is that he or she *never works for the buyer.* The agent may show buyers around, hold hands, present an offer, even hold the baby during the closing, but the agent is always paid by the seller out of the proceeds of the sale.

This holds true even for so-called "buyer's agents" who are more closely allied with buyers. A buyer's agent may help you negotiate a lower price, but the agent will still be paid out of the sale proceeds. Some agents, especially in a tough market, may work for the equivalent of an hourly fee to help prepare an offer, closing documents and the like. You can also hire a lawyer for that sort of service.

The basic buyer-agent-seller arrangement is built around a commission that typically equals about 6% of the total sale price. Yes, the seller pays the commission but, ultimately, it's the buyer who forks over the money. So, a smart buyer can turn that commission deal to his advantage.

That's because in a typical real-estate transaction, there are several characters standing in line with their hands out, beginning with the "listing" agent, the agent who has a contract to sell the property. If a buyer walks in with his own agent, the 6% commission is split between the two agents (the money is then further split between the individual agents and their bosses, the brokers, but that's not a big concern to the buyer or seller). So cut one of those players out. A buyer who deals with just the listing agent has a 3% price advantage over the competing buyer who is being squired around by another agent. When an agent won't have to split a commission, you can ask and sometimes they will offer to pay part of the price by giving back some commission.

Example: a seller insists on a $200,000 price, which includes a $12,000 real-estate commission. If you offer $197,000, the listing agent might be persuaded to throw in the additional $3,000.

With the advent of online house shopping—most notably *http://realtor.com,* the real-estate industry's own multiple-listing service open to the public—it's very easy for house shoppers to make a list of places they want to see, contact individual listing agents and arrange visits. Be aware, however, that some sellers—especially of expensive properties—may limit the commission if the agent represents both sides of the deal.

Whatever the case, having one less person getting a cut of the deal saves you money.

"strips," apartment blocks, single-family neighborhoods and industrial zones. Suburban developments built in the 1960s and '70s offer some of the more attractive deals these days, as the houses tend to be smaller and their styles quite out of fashion. (Don't let that bother you. Today's new homes will look quite out of fashion themselves in ten or twenty years. Besides, the mid-century ranch-style home of the 1960s is already popular with the vanguard design crowd, and '70s styles are quickly finding a new generation of fans.)

Roger Cruzen and his family found just such a neighborhood when they moved from Los Angeles to the Twin Cities ten years ago. They spent their first year renting and scoping out the area, and they found a 1960s neighborhood about twelve miles west of downtown Minneapolis, in the close-in, inner ring of suburbs that have gained popularity in metropolitan areas all over the country.

"It felt really good. It felt like this could be home," Roger recalls. "The kids were excited. We were excited. When we moved in, our neighbors brought us brownies."

HOW TO OWN A HOUSE

How you end up owning your home is every bit as important as how you buy it. This is especially important for unmarried and same-sex couples who buy property together.

With a house, unlike most other purchases, you don't just pay your money and take ownership. It matters *how* you take ownership—a.k.a. take "title" to your property. Very early in the process—in some states as early as when you make the initial offer—you will have to say how you plan to hold the property. There are tax and estate implications that you may not confront for decades, so get it right at the first.

Here are your choices:

Community property. This is the preferred method of ownership for married couples in community-property states, where each spouse owns what he or she had before the marriage and one-half of the property acquired during the marriage.

In general, both spouses have equal control how the property is managed, and if one spouse wants to hand over his or her interest to someone else, the other must agree. Also, either spouse can will his or her share to anyone he or she wants.

In California, couples, including same-sex couples who are registered as "domestic partners" may hold homes as community property.

Joint tenancy. In a joint tenancy, each owner has an "undivided" interest and "right of survivorship," meaning that if one owner dies, the other automatically becomes owner of the deceased owner's share. Outside community-property states, married couples and domestic partners usually hold properties as joint tenants, so that either spouse or partner will own the property completely when the other dies.

Tenants in common. Unrelated partners are far more likely to own properties as tenants in common, with each partner owning just a portion that is passed on to an estate upon the partner's death.

Warning: Don't just go for cheap. You can always improve a trashy property in an up-and-coming part of town, but your fixed-up house won't turn a trashy neighborhood into the new up-and-coming one. It's better to be the tenth or twentieth newcomer to a neighborhood that's already getting better than it is to be the first in a neighborhood that's not yet taken off.

Look at lots of places. Don't fall in love with a place you see your first Sunday afternoon of visiting open houses. Remember: it's a buyer's market out there, so never let anyone pressure you into making an offer right away.

Once you have settled on the area you want to be in, you will want to see as many houses as you can to be able to gauge for yourself what level of repair and amenities are good deals. How do you know what a $300,000 house looks like if you have seen only a couple?

That's what Andrew and Tina Coleman did when they decided to give up their 600-square-foot apartment in San Francisco. They cast their net wide and then gradually narrowed it. "We were spending all our weekends driving around the Bay Area," Andrew says.

The Colemans looked in the city itself and the northern suburbs across the Golden Gate before finally settling on the East Bay. They focused on a three-block area in the community of Piedmont. They liked the schools, the sense of community and the fact that there was a coffee shop and an ice-cream parlor within walking distance. It took them two years, but they eventually found a house they wanted in the neighborhood they wanted—a hillside, three-bedroom bungalow with a peek view of the Bay.

Whatever you do, don't make a firm offer on the first place you see—even if it meets every criterion you think you have. It's very easy to walk into a house with new countertops, refinished floors and new paint everywhere and feel it's all fixed up. Chances are it's not. Look at it without comparing it to other places, and you will end up not seeing the flaws and

HOW TO BUY A FORECLOSED HOUSE

 The very best way to get a house cheaply is to buy after it has been taken back by the bank. Here's a much simplified way to buy a foreclosed three-bedroom, two-bath house picked at random in the troubled Tampa area, but the basic strategy works everywhere. The worse the market, the better your chances of landing your dream home at a dream price.

Tampa's Hillsborough County has all kinds of public records online that anyone, anywhere can visit for free, including the county clerk's "lis pendens" (litigation pending) list. It's where the first official document in an impending foreclosure shows up. (Go to the county court clerk at *http://www.hillsclerk.com* and click "online searches.")

Wherever you are looking to buy, you should always go to a county clerk's office or Web site first, to see what foreclosure information is readily available. Or you can pay to get similar lists almost anywhere from pay services such as Realtytrac.com.

Listings give a basic description of the house, its location, the lender and the amount of the mortgage loan. For this house: $110,000, but anyone wanting to buy the house should be able to get it for well below that. Sophisticated buyers of foreclosed properties know that they—not the home owner, who is facing financial ruin, nor the lender about to take over the property—are in the driver's seat on such potential acquisitions. A buyer who is ready to make a deal can drive a hard bargain and make out very well. And the worse the market, the better for the buyer.

That's because by this point both the delinquent home owner and the mortgage holder are over barrels. The home owner is three months behind on his mortgage payments and could well be out of work and behind on lots of other bills as well. The house is getting shabbier daily as the owner saves money by not fixing things and not maintaining the lawn. He has probably been trying to sell the house but can't find a buyer.

Meanwhile, the lender has already lost at least three months of payments on this loan and now must wait out the home owner for an additional three to six months before it will be allowed to take over the property, after a public auction at which it will bid the value of the mortgage note.

point, the lender will take over the house, evict the former a quick fix-up, hire a real-estate broker and put it on the market there's an abundance of houses on the market and even the very ones are sitting unsold for months and months.

In other words, this lender is facing a year or more of lost income, back taxes and insurance, rehab costs, broker's fees and ongoing taxes, utility charges and maintenance expenses. And unlike a home owner or a landlord, the lender-owner facing losses can neither live in the house nor rent it out. This lender wants out.

That gives a potential buyer considerable clout with both the delinquent home owner and the lender. First, you'll want to approach the home owner, offering a "short sale"—which is a price below the existing mortgage balance. Depending on whether the owner has any equity (you'll know from your intelligence gathering how much; just compare the listed purchase price with the mortgage amount), the owner may or may not go for the initial idea.

The best deal you can expect from the home owner is to acquire the building for the cost of making the owner whole with the lender and any others with liens against the property—mainly the accumulated missed payments, just a couple of thousand dollars at this point. This is called a "subject to" purchase, and like any short-sale deal, it must be approved by the lender. (Although most mortgage contracts include "due on sale" clauses that require full repayment of the loan upon transfer to a new owner, many lenders will work with buyers who step in at this stage.)

If you simply make the owner whole and take over an existing 90% or 95% note, however, you won't make a good deal. You have to make a "short sale" offer—offer less money than the mortgage balance. The owner will need the lender's OK. If he doesn't get it, let the place go into foreclosure. The lender will take over the property at auction because no one is likely to bid more than the mortgage value. Then low-ball the lender.

Recognize that a foreclosed property is a lender's failure, and the managers want to get rid of it. The mortgage money has been written off, so all the bank really wants is to mitigate any further losses that it will incur holding on to the property.

Once the lender has taken over the property and evicted the former owner, it will place the property with the "REO" (real-estate owned) department for disposal. It will be listed with a local broker and put up for sale, usually at a price that will recoup a substantial portion of the bank's losses. There's nothing at all firm about that. A bank will entertain any reasonable offer. And in a historic down market such as the nation is now experiencing, a bank will entertain and accept plenty of unreasonable offers, too.

paying way too much for minimal aesthetic work that's been done.

After you have seen a few houses, revise your shopping list to fit the neighborhood. If you settle on an early '60s subdivision, you might find that breakfast nooks are pretty standard. But that half bath you wanted off the living room just isn't going to happen.

Learn about the house. Become a good reporter. Once you have a particular house in your sight, learn as much as you can about it. Learn about the seller, too.

At the very least, you can go to Internet sites such as Zillow.com, Trulia.com and PropertyShark.com and learn what you can about the house. At Zillow, for instance, you can look up past sales, tax assessments and the health of the overall local market (down to the zip code level). You can also find comparable sales information and other nearby homes for sale. At PropertyShark the information is much more specific (although far fewer areas are covered), including the amount of the mortgage and the name of the owners.

One bit of intelligence that you will find most useful: How long has the house been for sale? What was the original asking price?

Knock on the neighbors' doors. Ask them about the neighborhood, town government, anything to engage them in conversation and find out what you can about the area, the house and its current owners. Buying in California? Ask how the area fared in the last fire or earthquake. Florida? How's the local

FINDING FORECLOSURES

Freddie Mac and Fannie Mae both maintain extensive "REO" (real-estate owned) property lists, as does the Department of Housing and Urban Development (HUD). In addition, just about every large mortgage lender maintains REO lists that can be accessed through their Web sites. You'll have to root around, but the lists are there.

Here are some examples:

http://bankofamerica.reo.com/search/

http://mortgage.chase.com/pages/other/co_properties_landing.jsp

http://www.citimortgage.com/Mortgage/Oreo/SearchListing.do

http://www.countrywide.com/purchase/f_reo.asp

http://www.pasreo.com/pasreo/ (Wells Fargo)

http://www.banking.us.hsbc.com/HICServlet?cmd_PropertySearchDefault=cmd_PropertySearchDefault (HSBC)

http://www.ahmhomes.com/ (American Home Mortgage)

http://www.homesteps.com/hm01_1featuresearch.htm (Freddie Mac)

http://www.ocwen.com/reo/home.cfm

http://www.hud.gov/homes/index.cfm

http://www.fanniemae.com/homebuyers/homes/howto.jhtml (click "Fannie Mae Owned Property Search" link in left bar)

http://www.homesales.gov (other government-owned properties)

hurricane preparedness? Schools? Crime? Traffic? Major high-way construction planned?

People love to talk, and, as good newspaper reporters everywhere know, once you get them talking you'll be surprised at what they'll tell you. Be polite. Be the kind of person this person would want for a neighbor. Don't say negative things about the seller or spread rumors.

By being curious and listening, you might pick up some useful intelligence that will help you figure out just how "motivated" the sellers are. Are they divorcing? Has someone been laid off? Have they already moved and are carrying two mortgage payments as they try to sell? Don't just blurt out these kinds of sensitive questions directly. But listen for hints ("Well, we haven't seen *him* lately"), and if the neighbors seem to be telling you something obliquely, steer the conversation in the direction they seem to be heading.

If you are seriously considering making an offer, kick your information gathering up a notch and do an online background search on the sellers. Start with a simple search, and then take that up a level with a landlord's-style online screening. Dozens of companies perform such checks for $25 to $50 or so, and most can report back a basic profile in just moments. (For some companies, search "tenant background screening" at Yahoo! or Google.) Typical profiles include credit and rental histories, credit history, civil judgments and employment information. That kind of intelligence could be worth many times the cost of the screening. Knowing that a seller faces a number of past due bills or legal problems could save you thousands of dollars when you're negotiating.

The point is you can never know too much about the person you are negotiating with, and you can never have too much information about the house you're negotiating for. The more you know, the more information you have to leverage, the better the deal you will make for yourself.

Negotiate from *your* strengths. Let's see what you have going for you as you go into a house purchase: funds to make a substantial down payment, a lender ready to give you a mortgage, and thorough knowledge of the market, the neighborhood, the house itself and the seller.

What's the seller bringing to the table? A house that's worth much less than it was just a year ago and few prospects to sell it even at its much reduced price.

So, lowball. Amateur home owners, even those selling under duress, are notoriously difficult to deal with. They are likely to be too attached to their price and to the house. Be ready for that, and try to use this obstinacy to your advantage. The seller's going to concentrate on the price you offer, so be ready to overwhelm him with the terms. Remember: depending on how the seller has priced the house, you want to make an offer that will put you within striking distance of your goal—30% or more below the bubble-era peak.

Here's one way a deal could go down:

Let's follow Luke and Peggy, a couple of Manhattan transplants, who want to leave the city and move into their dream home in the country. They are eyeing a charming, restored 125-year-old farmhouse on five acres in a rural-turning-suburban Connecticut town on the far fringe of the New York metropolitan area. The seller is asking $359,000. According to Zillow, the house would have been valued at about $450,000 in 2005.

Luke and Peggy's goal is to get the house for about $315,000 (30% off the bubble-era value). They get ready to offer $250,000. (They know from their research that the price is still $100,000 more than the seller paid ten years ago when he bought it as a weekend-vacation home.)

First, Luke puts a call in to his banker, whom he and Peggy met on one of their house-hunting excursions to the town. Luke tells him they are preparing an offer and the price at which they expect the negotiations to settle out. They know they will be well within the bank's upper limit for them to borrow.

Luke also gives the banker the address of the house. "Oh yes," says the banker. "I know that place. Nice property. I haven't

A HOME-BUYING ALTERNATIVE

There is one way to take the lessons of professional property investing and management to heart when you buy your home. Share the burden. Buy an investment property to live in.

The best way to buy any property is to use other people's money to do it. That's what professional real-estate investors do—indeed, that's exactly how they earn their livings—and it's the only sure way for you, a home buyer, to reduce your expenses so much that you will make an actual profit on your home in just about any market. And a prudent income-property buyer can use his rental property to buy his move-up dream home and still have other people pay for it.

You can enter the home-buying cycle at the same late-twenties to early-thirties time period as other buyers but end up way ahead in your fifties and sixties. For a complete discussion of the finances and operation of small rental properties, see *The Wall Street Journal. Complete Real-Estate Investing Guidebook*. For now, however, here's the short version.

1. **But a two-, three- or four-unit property.** In most places in the country, multi-family buildings in good neighborhoods can be bought for about the same money as a single-family home. And loans for these types of properties are as easy to obtain as any mortgage if you have a substantial down payment, a good job and good credit. Lenders will even count the rental income toward determining your suitability for a loan.

2. **Live in one unit and rent the others.** Use the rental income along with the portion of your own income that you have set aside for housing payments to accelerate your mortgage payments. A $300,000, thirty-year mortgage will cost about $1,850 a month. Supplement that with an additional $1,800 of rental income, however, and you will pay the balance in less than ten years.

3. **Borrow against the income property.** Then, use that money to buy your dream home. If your move-up home is in the same price range as your investment property, you will need only a small first mortgage with a very low loan-to-value ratio (if at all), and your tenants will buy most of the house for you with their monthly rental payments.

been over that way in a while. I'll drive by on my way home this afternoon to give it a look."

At this point, Luke asks for an important assurance. As part of their offer, they want to give the seller a quick closing date. He asks the bank to fund the loan as quickly as possible. Two weeks? A month? Nothing longer than a month. The banker promises to get back to Luke the next day.

"Three weeks," the banker says in the morning. "Two if we can get the appraiser in the house by the weekend." The paperwork is in order and on hand, the down payment is on deposit at the bank, the background and credit checks are done, and the bank's preferred appraiser has a wide-open calendar (business has been slow lately), the banker says. He says he'll just fill in the blank when the price is agreed to and take the package to the loan committee (which consists of the loan officer himself, his branch manager and a guy from the finance department). Not a problem on that end.

Luke calls the seller's agent. "Two fifty," he says. "If we can get the appraiser in right away, we'll close in two weeks. All I want is an inspection, next week. If we find any problems, I'll want the seller to fix them or adjust the price."

"This is very low," says the agent. "I don't think he'll go for it."

"Try him," Luke answers back. "The clock's ticking. I'm on the bank's timetable now. They say it's either right away or we'll have to wait."

Luke and Peggy know that the agent must present the offer to the seller regardless of what the agent thinks the response may be. The seller needn't respond to an offer at all, but if he comes back with any kind of counteroffer—even if they are still far apart on the final price—then Luke and Peggy can be sure that they will be on their way to getting the house of their dreams at close to the price they want.

In this case, the seller, who hasn't had any kind of offer in a couple of months, does come back, at $330,000. Luke and Peggy counter at $290,000. The back and forth goes on, and everyone finally settles at $315,000, but with the seller paying the closing attorney, the inspection firm and giving back $3,500 for repairs (total: $5,000).

Luke and Peggy's bottom line? They get their new house right at their mark—$310,000, which is just 69% of the bubble-era value of $450,000.

This scenario is not at all far-fetched.

Sometimes it can be even better for the buyer. Indeed, if Luke and Peggy were really lucky, they would have been dealing with a mortgage company employee saddled with unloading this and other bubble-era mistakes made by the bank. He'd be in as big of a hurry as the buyers and ready to hear whatever they had to say. And unlike a home owner, a banker has no sentimental attachment to a house. It's his job to cut the bank's losses and unload the damn thing.

CHAPTER 6

SETTLING IN

I was simply furnishing a home. I love music . . . and I
don't think a $130,000 indoor-outdoor stereo system is
extravagant.

—LEONA HELMSLEY

Home buyers who entered the housing market well before the bubble can expect to profit from much of the era's price run-ups and not suffer so much of its fallout. If you're a pre-bubble buyer, your combined equity and appreciation—even post-bubble—should be substantial, especially if you bought your first home in the price trough that followed the housing boom of the 1980s.

Because you are unlikely to suffer from the kind of devastating value decline that early-cycle buyers are facing, you can choose to sell or to stay put without endangering your long-run financial well-being. If you try to sell and move up, you will face a sluggish market for your existing home, but that will be somewhat mitigated by excellent prospects for some good buys in the move-up market.

On the other hand, staying where you are means you can maintain and improve your house to meet your current and future needs and desires. That's what we're going to concentrate on in this chapter because doing so is more likely to result in greater long-term financial benefits for you. If you re-

BUT IF YOU DO WANT TO SELL AND MOVE UP . . .

You have two options if you are considering a move up. First, you can buy a new home if you have the cash and can afford to carry two residences for an indeterminate amount of time. Or more likely, you can move up if you can sell your existing house rather quickly for a price that doesn't eat into your equity from your original down payment and your principal payments over the years. You have worked hard to save that money, and you don't want to lose it.

As you crunch your numbers, don't count on your bubble-era appreciation. Think of that, instead, as your price cushion—at the best, a substantial premium that you may get when you sell, at worst maybe just enough to cover your real-estate agent's commission and moving costs.

Whatever you do, set a realistic, sellable price on day one. As we saw in chapter 5, smart buyers will be looking for bargains. So you must set your price 25% to 35% below the house's peak bubble value—or whatever the appropriate markdown is in your area.

Don't take my word for it. Use an online property evaluation site like Zillow or Trulia. Get a real-estate agent to suggest a price for you. Look at the asking prices and rental prices for comparable nearby properties. You could even pay to have an appraisal done. Just make sure your price is right, according to these outside sources. Don't fight the market by trying to price your house at bubble-era levels.

Unless you absolutely must move, don't just sell for the sake of moving or just because you think you can get a great deal on a newer, bigger place. That deal isn't as great as it seems because you're also giving someone a great deal on your current house.

If you can't get a price that recovers your equity, then stay where you are. You can always try again in a few years.

sist the urge to move too often, maintain your home well and are a smart renovator, you will retire your mortgage debt more quickly, spend less overall on housing, improve the quality and value of your home and have more money to make other, more lucrative investments.

CLEAN UP, PAINT UP, FIX UP

It's a throwback to the 1950s. Every March, the home owners of the Evergreen Historic District in Memphis, Tennessee, get together to spruce up their homes and the neighborhood. In Evans, New York, the town council has designated May as "Clean Up, Paint Up, Fix Up Month" and urges all residents to help out. In Live Oak, Texas, home owners are encouraged to clean out their garages and storage sheds as they buff up the town.

Yes, it does all sound a little corny and a bit Norman Rockwell–esque, but there is more than a grain of wisdom in the efforts. Nothing maintains property values better than owners who maintain their properties. Your house looks better if your neighbors' houses look good. And their houses look better if the street is clean, the sidewalks are swept and graffiti on the bus-stop shelter is quickly scrubbed away.

The primal force that real-estate agents earnestly call "pride of ownership"—the transformation of home owners into amateur landscape designers, painters, carpenters and cleaning crews—has the strongest impact on home values, next to school quality. Individually, the most important thing that any home buyer can do to protect the value of his biggest asset is to see that the house is always kept in good repair. The collective value of a neighborhood of attractive, well-maintained houses is greater than the sum of its individual properties. There's no price bonus for the best kept house on a shabby block.

Think of your house like anything else that gets left out in the rain. Do nothing to keep the elements at bay, and crabgrass will subsume the patio in a season while vines will blot out the view from the front porch by August. Put off pointing the chimney, and water will soak into and separate the plywood beneath the roof shingles. Let the leak beneath the sink go for a week or two, and black mold will spread out of sight behind the refrigerator. Without pride of ownership—that is without constant repair and maintenance—a house will collapse and decay and disappear back into nature in fifty years, posits writer Alan Weisman in his book *The World Without Us.* One hundred years, tops.

Your job as a home buyer and someday full-fledged home owner is to protect the money you have spent on your biggest asset, while making sure that the ceiling doesn't collapse on your sleeping kids. The best way to do that is with a continuous and systematic whole-house maintenance program. That is an expensive "I-have-to-pay-something" cost that can be mitigated but can't be ignored. Expect to pay up to 3% a year of your house's value on regular upkeep, repairs and special projects— everything from the weekly yard service to annual furnace checkups. You'll pay a lot more if you are renovating.

At the back of this book, you will find some helpful maintenance information. Appendix 1 is a list of expected lifetimes of various home elements prepared by the National Association of Home Builders. Appendix 2 is a home owner's annual maintenance checklist compiled by the Canada Mortgage and Housing Corp., a government agency roughly comparable to the U.S. government's Department of Housing and Urban Development. Both of these lists will be helpful as you map out your own maintenance program.

Here are a few broad repair and maintenance suggestions to get you started:

- **Have a regular team of repairmen.** You don't want to be interviewing plumbers on the phone as the water cascades from the ceiling. Start with a general handyman or contractor who can handle a broad range of jobs. Then ask him and your friends for the names of specialists. You'll need an electrician, a plumber, a carpenter and a painter. Try people out on small projects first. If you're satisfied with their work, put them on the permanent call list. Also, try to bundle similar jobs. Most repairmen charge $100 to $200 just to come to your house. They then charge for the job on top of that. If you have three plumbing jobs that can be done at once, you will save by paying only one basic charge.

- **Set up a maintenance fund.** You want to have $2,000 to $4,000 cash to cover emergency repairs and large occasional expenses. This could even be an account at your company credit union where they take out a little bit of money from every check. However you save the money, you want the cash on hand. You don't want to be on the hook to buy major household fixtures (think a furnace or a central air-conditioner compressor) on a credit card with an 18% interest rate. When you do have a major bill, be sure to replenish the account. You'll have yet another big-ticket repair soon enough.

- **Do what you can yourself.** Hiring a skilled tradesman will double the cost of any large project and turn a small job into an expensive one. Of course, you should hire professionals for dangerous or especially difficult jobs—you shouldn't re-roof your house, nor should you install a new electric panel—but most minor repair jobs around the house can be done by any competent adult. Don't be intimidated. Read and follow the instructions, get a good home-repair manual, and you can always take a home-maintenance class at a community college. (Two tips you'll thank me for later: turn off the water at the valve below the sink *before* you remove the faucet handle, and never, never replace a light switch until *after* you trip the circuit breaker.)

- **Have the right tools.** Nothing's more frustrating to a weekend repair warrior than to start a project and then realize an hour into it that you don't have a tool you need. Build yourself a good, basic collection of house and garden tools—hand and power. You don't need a lot, but you do

MR. AND MS. FIXIT

Here are the basic tools that any home owner needs in the utility closet. Everything on the list should total between $200 to $300, roughly equal to one plumber's visit:

Blue tape. Designed for masking between paint projects, but versatile and useful for other temporary taping jobs. It peels off easily.

Duct tape. The perfect fixer.

Flashlight. You don't have three hands when you need them, so get a light that stands by itself or hangs.

Hammer. A one-pound "claw" hammer with a fiberglass or wood handle.

Level. Scratch the lasers and stick to the old-fashioned "bubble" type, 24 inches.

Nails and screws. A wide assortment of various sizes. Always have plenty of $1\frac{1}{2}$-inch drywall screws.

Paintbrushes and rollers. Various sizes. Synthetic brushes are best for water-based paints; natural for oil-based paints. Use rollers with thick naps to paint rough surfaces; short for smooth.

Pliers. Mid-sized (8 inches) "slip-joint" pliers, "needle-nose" pliers and wire cutters.

Plunger. Saves lots of misery. If you have chronic toilet clogging problems, add a "closet" auger—the metal "snake" that plumbers use to clean drains.

Putty knife. Three or four in various sizes from 2 inches to 6 inches. And a small tub of spackle.

Safety goggles. And a collection of paper masks for painting and dusty jobs.

Sandpaper. An assortment.

Saws. A crosscut hand saw for small wood-cutting projects. A hacksaw cuts metal.

Screwdrivers. Six to eight in various sizes of both—most important— the flat- and Phillips-head types. A cordless electric screwdriver will save you lots of backaches, but it won't be powerful enough for the harder jobs; an electric drill with screwdriver heads will work better.

Tape measure. A twenty-five-foot tape is pretty standard. Remember: measure twice, cut once.

Toolbox or bucket. Keep everything in one place. Even more frustrating than not having the right tool is having it and not finding it.

Wrenches. A basic set will have eight to ten of various sizes. Also a couple of adjustable wrenches, one of which should be large enough to grip the fittings of the U-shaped "trap" pipe under a bathroom or kitchen sink.

need more than just a hammer, some pliers and an electric drill. For onetime or once-a-year projects, you should rent or borrow what you need. Most good hardware stores have tool-rental departments, and a few towns around the country have tool libraries where you can borrow tools for specific projects (here's one: *http://www.westphillytools.org/*).

- **Be a good neighbor.** Two or three sets of hands can make the most difficult jobs much easier. Offer to help your neighbors with their routine repair projects, and they will pay you back with their aid when you need it. Again, avoid jobs that should be handled by professionals (unless, of course, your neighbor happens to be a licensed electrician), but even a couple of middle-management marketers should be able to caulk some windows or clean out gutters. Start a "clean up, paint up, fix up" program with your friends, and before long you might get the whole neighborhood involved.

Don't get carried away. Maintenance is one thing; it's necessary, there's no way to get around it, and you can't really go overboard. But pride of ownership can have a dark side, too.

HOME DIS-IMPROVEMENT

Certainly the most frequent and expensive efforts that mid-cycle home buyers put into their homes are renovations—some minor, many quite elaborate. What Americans spend on their homes *after* buying them is mind-boggling. There's no one set of numbers, but various sources suggest that the nation's annual home-improvement bill—do-it-yourself and hired remodeling, landscaping and major repair projects—could be $400 billion or more. That's $300 a month for every household in the country.

Not surprisingly, entire industries have arisen to get their pieces of the action. Magazines and television programs entice home owners to spend tens of thousands of dollars for new kitchens with custom-built cabinets, granite countertops and designer appliances. Architects and builders woo clients with bedrooms that have swollen into his-and-hers master suites with separate dressing rooms, sitting rooms and exercise areas. Simple bathrooms have become spas featuring expensive electronic toilets, multihead showers and Asian-inspired "soaking" tubs. Landscapers construct elegant "outdoor rooms" that feature dining and lounging areas, even kitchens, that are the equals of comparable rooms inside the house.

Unfortunately, the "home as investment" mind-set encourages owners to spend money on these kinds of expensive upgrades to boost the home's resale price and to stay even with the rest of the houses in the neighborhood. Ask any home owner why he or she is remodeling and fairly quickly you'll hear: "It will increase the value of the house."

Doug Guillaume, the former New Orleans home owner-turned-Houston renter whom we met in chapter 5, recalls the $10,000 or so that he spent on new flooring and renovating a bathroom. He did much of the work himself, and remembers looking at much more ambitious and expensive projects at his neighbors' homes.

"When I talked to people around me," Doug says, "they were renovating a lot more than I was. I thought, *There's no way you're making money on your house.* I never figured out how they were doing it. How can you make money on this?"

RENOVATE AND REPAIR

Whether you are planning to sell in the next few months or stay put until your old age, a smart home improver will make sure to combine home repairs with home renovations. It goes back to what the government allows you to include in the "cost basis" of the house. That's the value of the house and improvements that you may deduct from the sale price when figuring your tax-free capital gain.

Repairs and replacements don't count. Renovating and remodeling do.

Always combine the two. Painting your house won't count as an improvement, but repainting the house at the same time that you add a bedroom wing will. Replacing a furnace won't contribute to your cost basis, but installing a new heating and air-conditioning system will.

They probably didn't. Reality check: renovating *might* increase the price of your house, but it's most often a fool's bet because few home improvements break even, much less make a profit. Like new cars, most home improvements are lousy investments, losing one-fifth or more of the cost the day the contractor finally loads up and leaves.

"I know that my return on investment could have been worse—even negative!—if I had not done most the renovations myself," says Doug. "I could have just rented and invested the difference in Treasury bills without making one trip to Home Depot."

Of course, there are varying degrees of remodeling, and some has to be done whatever the cost and the potential for

GOING GREEN

It should be clear by now to any home-owning U.S. citizen that conservative, thrifty usage of Earth's resources is smart finance, good stewardship and sound foreign policy. It's not often that the right thing to do also happens to be the most economical.

As you plan home projects, remember that economies are realized over the long term and not just the short. Products that are cheaper to buy often turn out to be far more expensive to own. A simple 75-watt incandescent lightbulb, for instance, may cost just 50 cents at the hardware store, but you will need thirteen of them to match the lifetime of one $5 compact fluorescent bulb (CFL). The incandescent bulbs will need $33 more electricity over 11,000 or so hours than the CFL bulb will burn.

Here are some financially savvy, environmentally helpful home-remodeling suggestions from "Designing and Building a More Sustainable Home," a brochure prepared by the City of Portland (Oregon) Office of Sustainable Development:

Reduce construction waste. Save and reuse whatever old materials from your house that you can, including old cabinets, floorboards, even lumber. Construction debris is 25% of the garbage in Portland's landfills, and that's less than most other big cities.

Conserve natural resources. See that your contractor uses recycled materials whenever possible. There is an expanding range of green building materials from which to choose, including decking, insulation, concrete drywall, fiberboard, tile, flooring and paint.

Improve indoor air quality. Many interior-design features are made with noxious, dangerous chemicals such as formaldehyde and "volatile organic compounds." These are thought to contribute to asthma and other respiratory problems. Insist on safer materials and see that your design includes adequate ventilation.

Save energy and water. Install energy-efficient Energy Star appliances and use alternative energy sources whenever possible.

Landscape with native grasses and plants that require fewer
chemicals and less water.

Reduce monthly costs. A remodel that includes energy-efficient
lights and appliances, weatherization and efficient space and water
heating can cut energy use in half compared to a conventional house.

return. All properties, for example, need maintenance and repairs, and it's not discretionary to fix a broken window, replace
a worn-out furnace, or sometimes even to add a new bathroom. The buyer of a fixer-upper with a kitchen that hasn't
seen a paintbrush or a scouring pad since 1967 doesn't have a
choice but to renovate. And a growing family has to do *something* when the kids are sleeping in the dining room because
the living room is already taken.

Other projects, however, balloon far beyond financial
common sense. Home owners are usually warned about "over-
improving" their property—making improvements that push
a house too far out of line with what other nearby properties
have—but they are rarely warned about the perils of remodeling by refinancing long-term mortgages. Nor are they warned
about improving beyond what they can reasonably expect to
recoup when they sell the place.

Remodeling, a trade magazine for builders, publishes a
widely quoted annual survey of the value of home improvements. The surveys are not perfect, but they are the best, most
widely available assessments of what's popular in home renovations and the only serious efforts to gauge the financial impact that various projects have on the resale value of homes.

The surveys are depressing. They lay bare the financial
fantasies that most home owners have when it comes to renovations and upgrades. Here are some samples:

REMODELING'S 2007 COST VERSUS VALUE REPORT

	Job cost	Resale value	Cost recouped
Midrange			
Attic bedroom remodel	$46,691	$35,771	77%
Back-up power generator	$13,357	$7,748	58%
Basement remodel	$59,435	$44,661	75%
Bathroom addition	$37,202	$24,553	66%
Bathroom remodel	$15,789	$12,366	78%
Deck addition—wood	$10,347	$8,835	85%
Family room addition	$78,989	$54,148	69%
Garage addition	$53,897	$37,461	70%
Home office remodel	$27,193	$15,498	57%
Major kitchen remodel	$55,503	$43,363	78%
Master suite addition	$98,863	$68,172	69%
Minor kitchen remodel	$21,185	$17,576	83%
Roofing replacement	$18,042	$12,166	67%
Siding replacement	$9,910	$8,245	83%
Sunroom addition	$69,817	$41,231	59%
Two-story addition	$139,297	$103,010	74%
Window replacement—vinyl	$10,448	$8,290	79%
Window replacement—wood	$11,384	$9,241	81%
Upscale			
Bathroom addition	$73,145	$50,442	69%
Bathroom remodel	$50,590	$34,588	68%
Deck addition—composite	$15,039	$11,672	78%
Garage addition	$82,108	$53,056	65%
Major kitchen remodel	$109,394	$81,096	74%
Master suite addition	$220,149	$141,120	64%
Roofing replacement—steel	$33,151	$21,769	66%
Siding replacement—fiber-cement	$13,212	$11,633	88%
Siding replacement—foam-backed vinyl	$12,132	$9,668	80%

	Job cost	Resale value	Cost recouped
Upscale *(continued)*			
Window replacement—vinyl	$13,479	$10,913	81%
Window replacement—wood	$17,383	$13,784	79%

Imagine the looks of horror you'd earn from your friends if you dropped this *bon mot* at a dinner party: "Sub Zeros are nice, but if you really want to get the most bang for your buck, go with the fiber-cement siding."

The point is that most remodeling has gone far off the scale of reasonableness, especially when the principal justification for most remodeling projects is financial. Why in the world would anyone borrow $109,000 to build a magazine-style kitchen when they can expect to recoup only 74% of the cost? Why in the world would anyone borrow the money and end up paying $100,000 more just in interest? What kind of investment is that?

That's not to say that people shouldn't ever renovate—families grow and most people will need more space or they'll want to make their home nicer. But you want to be very smart about remodeling. The first thing you should ask yourself . . .

WHY ARE YOU REMODELING?

To accommodate a growing family? To put the house up for sale? To make an old house more modern? To give yourself a treat? To adapt the house to your own changing living requirements?

Each of these is a perfectly good, perfectly valid reason to renovate. Just don't let your desires get so far ahead of your checkbook that there is no sound financial justification for your project. You can't expect to make a profit on a home remodel, and, over time, the value of the improvement declines or, at best, is simply subsumed into the house value. Think of it this way: a twenty-year-old kitchen remodel is not going to push up the value of your home. Keep these points in mind:

- **Balance your wants with your needs.** Your expectations must fit your budget so that when you start planning a remodel or renovation, you don't wind up with every expensive accessory or item in the architect's or builder's inventory. Custom-built kitchen cabinets, granite countertops and top-of-the-line, restaurant-style appliances look fantastic, but there are plenty of more modest and affordable alternatives. You may need or just want a new kitchen or a new bathroom or a new master closet, but that doesn't mean you need every high-end accessory or appliance that can go into it. In any room you are renovating, always go with the least that you want and the most that you need.

- **Don't try keeping up with the neighbors.** Unless you are fixing up your house to put it up for immediate sale, there is no valid financial argument for remodeling just to keep your home improvements on a par with your neighbors'. And if you are renovating to sell, keep your expenses to a minimum. Unless you can expect that a specific buyer will pay more for a major renovation than it costs, you can't justify the expense financially. You lose money if you spend $50,000 improving a $300,000 house so you can put it up for sale at $345,000. Inexpensive new carpets, new paint and fresh flowers in the window boxes will spruce up the house nicely and catch the eye of a buyer for a fraction of the cost of a major remodel.

- **Consider the lifetimes of improvements.** Houses are not fashionable outfits to be worn and discarded after just a season or two, and home improvements are too expensive to be treated like last year's dress. It wasn't so very long ago that the well-renovated home had to have built-in Ethernet wiring for room-by-room Internet access. And it was even more recently that wireless Internet access rendered all those wired connections quaint, if not altogether obsolete. Today's hot new technological innovations—think of those big-screen TVs that are sprouting on the walls of your friends' reconfigured and rewired family rooms—will be supplanted by some other technological innovation soon enough. It's the same with major architectural elements— just ask someone who's paying today's oil prices to heat a two-story entry foyer.

- **Look for the no-brainer economies.** Yes, you can buy the cheaper hardware, but your big savings will come in cutting your labor costs. So, get out your ratty clothes, pick up a hammer and get to work. There are plenty of remodeling jobs that anyone can do, from knocking down walls to cutting and stapling insulation battens to hanging drywall to tiling and painting. Save the difficult, dangerous or expensive stuff for the pros, but you should be able to trim a substantial portion of your renovation costs by doing whatever work you can yourself. The more work you do, the more money you will save.

- **Avoid long-term borrowing.** You wouldn't buy a car with a thirty-year loan, and you shouldn't add a bathroom that way, either. Home improvements should be paid for out of pocket or with only short-term (less than five years) loans. Not only is that the best way to keep yourself from spending too much money, it's the only way to keep your losses from spiraling way beyond reason. Remember: you are losing money going into the project, and you don't want to increase your losses by paying years and years of interest as well. That new $73,000 upscale bathroom could end up costing you more than $150,000 if you pay for it with a new thirty-year first mortgage or home-equity loan. Pay for it over just five years, and you will still be out almost $87,000. (One big exception to this rule: if you are undertaking a whole-house remodel in lieu of buying a new place. That can be a good move if values have increased enough that your now new house won't be too expensive for the neighborhood.)

With these points in mind, let's look at some of the kinds of home-improvement projects that make financial sense for home buyers who will live in their houses for many years.

Bedrooms. New bedrooms are a utilitarian, inexpensive addition to a home, especially if a growing family is bursting at the house seams. As a rule, however, additions that increase the overall floor space of a house are not as cost effective as re-allocating the existing footprint. There is an exponential increase in remodeling costs once you push beyond the existing house envelope and roofline. And often there is no need to.

For example, the difference between a two-bedroom house with a den and a three-bedroom house usually comes down to a closet. Bedrooms have closets; dens don't. Enclose a few square feet with a simple wall and a door (about $1,500 if you hire someone), and you will have a third bedroom in just a couple of days. Similar retrofitting can be conducted in dining rooms or living rooms—or any room of the house that is underused. Should you ever want to reclaim the room for its original use, any of the work can be undone just as quickly when the kids move out.

Expensive bedroom additions can also be avoided by reconfiguring the existing layout of the house—covered porches, attics and storage areas as well as existing rooms. In modern homes, for instance, secondary bedrooms are about 150 square feet. In contrast, the second bedroom in a 1950s home was only about 100 square feet. Do the math: parents in the 1950s could raise three Baby Boomers (more if they doubled up) in the same space as parents today raise two kids. Similarly, large master bedrooms, which are typically about 260 square feet, can be reconfigured into two rooms with minimal structural work.

Although it's easy and economical to reconfigure non-load-bearing walls, even the more expensive rebuilding of

REMODELING FOR A LIFETIME

One area of economical remodeling that is gaining interest is "universal design." That's building and remodeling to better accommodate seniors and people with disabilities.

If you're planning to stay in your home well into old age, it would be smart to plan for it as you tackle renovation projects.

If you are healthy in your fifties or sixties, there's no need to go all the way. Just incorporate universal-design principles in your remodeling projects. Then, when you do get older, you will need to have less work done to fit the house to your situation.

Kansas State University has a simple home "universal design" checklist. It's available at *http://www.oznet.ksu.edu/library/HOUS2/MF2213.pdf*.

Here are some of the high points:

- Doors should be at least 32 inches wide to allow for wheelchair access; lever-type handles rather than round knobs.

- Light switches should be 36 to 42 inches from the floor.

- One grade-level entrance to the house or room for a ramp with no greater than a 1:12 rise (1 foot up every 12 feet).

- Front-loading washer and dryer on the main living level, not down in the basement.

- Kitchen cooktops should be 30 inches to 32 inches from the floor, slightly lower than standard counter height, with control knobs in the front or sides.

- Wall-mounted ovens and a side-by-side refrigerator.

- Pull-out shelves on lower cabinets.

- Lever-type faucets in both the kitchen and the bathroom.

- A handheld European-style showerhead; a built-in seat in a stall shower or tub.

load-bearing structural walls (walls that carry the weight of the exterior walls and roof) can be carried out far cheaper than building a separate addition.

Bathrooms. Like bedrooms, bathrooms that can be added within the existing footprint of a house are far cheaper than building new. Where the cost of remodeling or adding a bathroom can take off, however, is in configuring the plumbing—that is the plumbing you don't see.

Unfortunately, there's no getting around it. Underneath the floor and behind the walls, the fanciest magazine-worthy bath and the humblest water closet look pretty much alike: a couple of supply pipes to bring water in and waste pipes to take it out, so you'll want to use as much of what's already there as you can. Look for places to add your new bathroom where the pipes are already in place or at least close enough that the plumbers can tap in to them easily. Ideally, that would mean converting a portion of a bedroom or a large closet adjacent to an existing bath.

By cutting your bathroom infrastructure costs, which no one sees, you'll enable yourself to splurge more on the fixtures that you and your guests do see. Once the pipes and drains are in, it costs no more to install a $500 lavatory than a $200 one.

A caveat: Bathrooms are much easier and cheaper to add to an existing floor plan if you are building on the second floor or the first floor of a house with a basement. You don't want to go tearing up a slab foundation, in which the waste pipes are embedded in concrete. It might be more economical in that case to build outside the existing footprint.

Kitchens. When it comes to home remodeling, kitchens are the main attraction and the biggest cost center. No other room is more susceptible to fads and fashions and, as a result, budget bloat.

A kitchen in a typical 1950s home was about 160 square feet and housed, along with the usual appliances, a washer and dryer and the family's main dining table. Today, a common kitchen floor plan devotes about 150 square feet to the principal work

FIVE QUICK AND CHEAP WAYS TO UPGRADE A KITCHEN

Renovating to sell? The kitchen is probably the most important room of the house to buyers. It's also the most expensive to upgrade.

Real-estate broker Barbara Corcoran has built a new career since selling her New York City agency in 2001 for $70 million. Now among her other projects, she dispenses advice to home buyers and owners at *http://barbaracorcoran.com*.

Here's her short, cheap way to fix up a kitchen:

1. **Replace the cabinet hardware.** You can give perfectly fine but outdated cabinets a new look by replacing the door and drawer pulls for about $1 each.

2. **Paint.** A fresh coat of paint will give a bright and airy feel. If the cabinets are dark, paint them white. White kitchens never go out of style.

3. **Replace the light fixture.** A simple yet updated replacement fixture can add new style for about $25 to $50. You can still be eco-friendly with a compact fluorescent bulb in your new light.

4. **Replace or create a backsplash.** Give your old tile backsplash a good scrub and a coat of white over the grimy grout. If you don't have a tile backsplash, consider installing one, or go with a few sheets of stainless steel.

5. **Updating appliances.** Replacing them is expensive. But updating isn't. Appliance refinishers will re-enamel a refrigerator or oven door with a stylish color for about $150.

area, another 150 to the "breakfast" area and another eighty or so to the laundry room.

The kitchen is the room most highly valued by home buyers and, to hear their laments and the laments of their designers, there's never been one properly designed. Although the soul

ADDING UP THE COSTS

The actual costs of home appliances—washers, dryers, dishwashers, refrigerators and the like—should be computed by combining their purchase price, any interest if you pay over time, plus fuel and operating expenses, all amortized over the expected life of the unit.

Let's say, for example, that Mary, a home owner in Texas, is shopping to replace her old refrigerator. She finds a stylish 25-cubic foot, side-by-side, model for $2,399, including tax, delivery, installation and haul off of her old unit. She will buy it with the store's own five-year, 14.99%, in-house credit deal. The yellow "Energy Guide" label says the unit will use about 633 kWh/year of electricity (less than half the electricity of the 1990s model she's replacing), at what the Department of Energy says is the average Texas rate of 12.86 cents per kWh. According to the Association of Home Appliance Manufacturers, Mary can expect her new refrigerator to have a useful life of fourteen years. Finally, let's say that over the course of fourteen years, she will have two $200 repairs—replacing the ice maker and the door seal.

What will Mary actually pay for her new refrigerator? $4,963—about $30 a month or $1 a day for the life of the unit—more than double what she thinks she's paying, with virtually all of the increase coming in interest and energy costs.

A New Refrigerator

Price	$2,399
Interest	$1,025
Energy	$1,140
Repairs	$400
TOTAL	**$4,963**
Per year	$355
Per month	$30

Refrigerators are notorious energy burners, but they are hardly the only ones in the typical American home. A dishwasher will consume half the energy of a refrigerator even though it runs no more than an hour or two each day. A washer and dryer together are likely to consume more electricity in a year than an efficient refrigerator.

of kitchen design has long been the so-called "triangle" plan—in which the stove, the refrigerator and the sink are the points of an equilateral triangle defining the room's primary workspace and work pattern—kitchen re-designers inevitably find that the triangle of an existing kitchen is wrong and must be reconfigured. That usually results in the expensive relocating of vents, plumbing, gas lines and electrical service. Add in the cost of stylish new appliances, special lighting and exotic countertops and cabinet materials, and remodeling costs can quickly soar beyond financial reason.

Control your spendthrift desires. Remember: balance your wants with your needs. An upscale remodel paid for with long-term borrowing can end up costing more than $200,000—enough to eat at the fanciest restaurant in town every week for twenty years. (Better cooking, too, most likely.)

As with bathrooms, economical kitchen remodeling uses the existing infrastructure. Whenever you can, renovate within the current footprint of the kitchen. Cabinets and islands can be reconfigured far easier than walls. The odds are that the work triangle that suited the previous owner and has suited you up until now will continue to work for you in your newly remodeled kitchen. Concentrate your energy and money, instead, on elements that will improve the utility of the kitchen and update its aesthetics:

- **Appliances.** Unless you are Emeril Lagasse, you should ask yourself whether you really need the $4,000 restaurant-style range. Seriously fashionable appliances will look quite dated long before they stop working. Cutting-edge glassy black appliances of the 1980s gave way to industrial stainless steel in the 1990s, which is now being supplanted at the high end of the design world by bright, high-gloss primary colors. This, too, shall pass. Somebody once liked avocado, too. Concentrate on classic styles and colors. A top-of-the line stainless steel General Electric range costs more than $2,000—25% to 35% more than a comparable top-of-the line white range. And don't feel that you need the latest technology and features, either. If you've never mastered your DVD player, you're no more likely to figure out all the controls on a pricey high-tech dishwasher.

- **Cabinets.** You can reface cabinets with new doors, hardware and veneers for less than half the cost of buying new ones, and you can refinish your existing cabinets for even less. Most kitchen remodelers end up ripping out, discarding and replacing perfectly fine cabinets when all they really need to get the look they want is to put on new doors and drawer fronts. Most of this is the kind of job that anyone with modest tool-wielding skills can accomplish in a weekend or two. And you can hire someone to do what you can't. The costs in time and money will still be far below a complete remodel. You can reconfigure your cabinets and add new, different types of storage units. Any good cabinet shop will be able to match what you have.

- **Countertops.** If you have economized on the appliances and the cabinets, countertops can be a good place to splurge. A nice, high-quality countertop raises the overall look of a kitchen, regardless of the cabinet that stands under it. Consider the countertop material's durability and maintenance requirements as well as price. And there's no set rule for costs. Prices run the entire range, from just $16 or so per lineal foot (that's 1 foot running and 2 feet deep) for Formica-type laminates to $400-a-foot ultra-high-end special stones.

SAVING DOLLARS, HOUR BY HOUR

With the price of oil fluctuating so wildly, any remodeling or renovations of your home should be undertaken with current and future energy and utility costs in mind. An American home owner can easily spend more than $400 a month for electricity, gas, water and sewer—much more if you're heating a New England farmhouse in January or air-conditioning an Arizona tract home in August.

You're not likely to ever cut your energy costs to zero, of course, but you can reduce expenses substantially over time by replacing home systems and employing alternative energy sources, replacing older appliances with more efficient models and using more up-to-date building techniques and materials for alterations to the house itself.

Although energy upgrades aren't likely to elicit the oohs and ahs of your friends—not many neighbors are going to come over to check out your new on-demand water heater or super-efficient refrigerator—they are the kind of unseen home upgrades that pay off for home owners who plan on staying in their homes for a long time.

We won't try to be all encompassing here, but we will look at some representative items to show how judicious upgrades can improve your personal bottom line. (For a comprehensive guide to home energy issues, get a copy of the "Consumer Guide to Home Energy Savings," produced by the American Council for an Energy-Efficient Economy. They also have an excellent Web site: *http://aceee.org.*)

You will also want to investigate any money-saving and energy-saving programs—including tax and utility-bill rebates— that are available where you live. Since 1995, the North Carolina Solar Center and the Interstate Renewable Energy Council have maintained the Database of State Incentives for Renewables & Efficiency (DSIRE)—a comprehensive and constantly updated compilation for all fifty states and U.S. territories. The volume of information is impressive—from $400 insulation rebates from the Blue Grass Energy Cooperative in Kentucky to South Dakota property-tax exemptions for renewable energy systems such as wind-power turbines and solar water heating. You can find the database at: *http://www.dsireusa.org/.*

Heating systems. Heating is the big energy hog. A home owner with an older furnace or boiler in New England or the Midwest can spend $1,000 a month from October through April. If your unit is older than twenty years, you can expect substantial savings by replacing it with a newer, more efficient model.

Easy savings: never buy in the winter. Shop for a new furnace in the spring or summer, when demand is low and prices are marked down. And, of course, you never want to be shopping for a furnace *after* the old one breaks down.

When shopping, know that it's all about a unit's "efficiency." That's measured as the annual fuel utilization efficiency (AFUE), expressed as a percentage. Furnaces range from 78% to 96%, but you should concentrate on "condensing" or two-stage furnaces that are rated 90% or above. You can measure your savings with this chart from the American Council for an Energy-Efficient Economy.

To determine your annual dollar savings, find the AFUE of your existing system and go across to the rating of the new system. The dollar figure is the savings per $100 of fuel. So if your hot-air heating system has an AFUE of 65% and you're spending $500 a month through the winter, a new $4,000 unit (including installation) with an AFUE of 90% will save you

	AFUE OF NEW SYSTEM			
	80%	85%	90%	95%
50%	$37	$41	$44	$47
55%	$31	$35	$38	$42
60%	$25	$29	$33	$37
65%	$19	$23	**$27**	$32
70%	$12	$18	$22	$26
75%	$6	$11	$17	$21
80%		$6	$11	$16
85%			$6	$11

AFUE OF EXISTING SYSTEM

$135 a month. Project that over a seven-month heating season, and you are looking at a substantial $945 a year. And the return on your investment (ROI) comes to: $4,000 ÷ $945 = 23.6%! Not bad. Wall Street should do so well. The new furnace will pay for itself in about four years.

Cooling systems. What heating costs do to home owners in Maine and Minnesota, air-conditioning can do to owners in Arizona and Florida. You could say Sun Belt summer cooling costs are going through the roof, but you'd want to make sure the roof is tightly sealed to make sure none of that expensive cold air is leaking out.

Central air conditioners and air-source heat pumps are both used in the United States, with air-conditioners performing best in the hot, dry climates of the Southwest and heat pumps taking the honors in hot, humid areas such as the Southeast (where heat pumps are also good for heating). Both are given a "seasonal energy efficient ratio" (SEER); the higher the SEER, the more efficient the cooler. Look for systems rated 14.5 or higher in humid climates, 15 in dry.

As long as you are putting in a new system, spend a bit more for one that uses R-410A refrigerant (sold under the name Puron and others). Older units use R-22 refrigerant, Freon, which causes serious damage to the atmosphere. Beginning in 2010, no new air-conditioning units using R-22 will be sold, but Freon will still be available for repairs to older systems.

Water heaters. Water heating is typically the third biggest energy user in a home, after heating and cooling. Water heaters are rated by their "energy factor" (EF), which indicates energy efficiency based on the amount of hot water produced per unit of fuel consumed; typical ratings range from .60 for a conventional gas heater with a tank to 1.20 for a solar heater with electric backup. Generally speaking, the most efficient and economical water heating systems are "indirect" or "integrated" systems that combine house heating with water heating, electric heat pump heaters that use one-third to one-half as much electricity as conventional electric heaters, solar heaters (especially in the South and West) and "demand" or "tankless" heaters that do not store water but heat it as it's required. Among the more traditional storage types of heaters, gas and propane heaters are far more economical than electric.

Windows. If you think of windows as big holes where air passes through the sides of your house, then you can imagine the kind of impact they have on your heating and cooling costs. Look for windows certified by the National Fenestration Rating Council, which rates the energy attributes of windows on a five-feature system. You will see the numbers on the council's labels affixed to windows, whether custom-made or the stock kind you find in home improvement stores. Here's how to read them:

- On a scale from .20 to 1.20, *U-value* measures how well the window keeps heat from escaping. The lower the number the better.

- *Solar heat gain coefficient* describes how much solar energy is transmitted through a window. Windows with high coefficients are designed for colder climates; low coefficients are for hotter areas.

- There's heat and there's light. The 0 to 1 *visible light transmittance* scale measures the relative amount of sunlight that can pass through. A higher number means more light.

- You want a low *air leakage* rating. That shows how much air passes through the cracks in the window assembly. The number represents the cubic feet of air passing through 1 square foot of window each minute.

- A window's *condensation resistance* is the measure of its durability. The 0 to 100 scale rates the window's ability to keep water from forming on the inside. You want a high number.

CHAPTER 7

FREE AND CLEAR

A man builds a fine house; and now he has a master, and
a task for life; he is to furnish, watch, show it, and keep it in
repair, the rest of his days.

— RALPH WALDO EMERSON

If you are a late-cycle home buyer or home owner who is retired or close to retirement, then you are facing many years of expenses and uncertain income. Yes, you are probably doing some part-time work, and yes, you have built up a nice retirement fund, and yes, you have Social Security and maybe you even have a traditional pension. But will all that be enough to live comfortably for the next twenty, thirty, even forty years?

If you are like most older Americans, a great portion of your wealth is tied up in your home. Too much, really. Typically, all but the very wealthiest Americans have much more than half of their net worth (that's all assets minus all debts) in their residences and other hard assets. And the real-estate portion of a household's net worth tends to increase in retirement as home owners spend down their savings and tap their investment accounts.

Understandably, then, more and more older Americans have come to look at their biggest asset as a source of retirement cash. Wrongheaded as the idea may have been, most of today's late-cycle owners probably started on their career paths with the idea that they would buy a home, build their house wealth through their working years, and then, someday, somehow, tap their equity and appreciation in their retirement years. For some, the dream is to sell the big, expensive family home, move to a retirement town somewhere high on the "places rated" hot list, pocket some dough and play golf for twenty years. For others, the dream may be to stay right where they have always been but have some extra money to travel or to enjoy some creature comforts they couldn't have when they were raising their families.

Whatever your picture of the perfect retirement, in this chapter we'll look at some of the ways you can extract money out of your home—to *monetize,* as financial types say, the home that you have put thirty years of savings into.

But first, you'll need to answer an important question. . . .

WHAT DO YOU WANT YOUR HOUSE TO BE?

That's easy, right? You want you house to be your house.

Financially, though, it's much more difficult to answer. Now, for the first time in this book, we *are* going to look at your home as a savings account. Certainly, we're going to look at your home as a potential source of money for you. So the question of what you want your house to be is important because it will determine how you can most efficiently realize the value of your home owner's nest egg.

So, what *do* you want your house to be? What kind of asset do you want? A source of income that you can use now and over the next three or four decades? Do you want to hold your house as a super reserve fund that will be available for you when you are really old and less able to handle your own affairs? Or do you simply want to pass your house on to your heirs as part of your estate?

Each choice carries its own set of issues and its own solutions, all of which will be affected by the downturn in real-estate

BEFORE YOU RETIRE

You must figure out how dependent your retirement is on your home. To do that, use a standard Web-based net-worth calculator, such as this one: *http://www.smartmoney.com/worksheets/*.

You want to see just what you have in financial assets—long-term savings, stock accounts, retirement funds and the like. Don't fill in the value of your home, car or other hard assets. And for good measure, don't include any cash in your checking or short-term savings accounts because that is money that is earmarked for spending not for saving.

Add up all your financial assets. Then add up whatever debts you have, including you mortgage balance if you still have one. Next, subtract your debts from your assets. Hopefully, you have a large, positive number. Then, multiply that number by .04 (4%), which is about what you can expect to take out every year without eating into your principal. (Some financial planners say you should count on only a conservative 3.5% income stream, so multiply by .035 if you want to be cautious.)

Finally, go to the Social Security Web site (*http://www.ssa.gov/planners/calculators.htm*) and use the quick calculator there to figure out what your benefit will be in inflation-adjusted dollars. Add that to your income from your financial assets. That's how much you can expect to live on every year of your retirement.

Most of us don't have nearly enough to live on as we'd like.

If you made $80,000 a year while working, just to maintain the median U.S. household income—about $45,000—you would need Social Security plus about $500,000 in financial assets. To maintain an income at what you are accustomed to, you'd need well over $1 million in retirement savings.

Remember: this is all savings independent of your home, which for the vast majority of owners is unlikely to be worth anywhere near $1 million.

Adding further insult: you will still have to live somewhere. And though you were smart and paid off your mortgage before you retired, all your other "I-have-to-pay-something" costs will keep going on and keep going up. Live for another thirty years in retirement, and you could end up buying your house all over again just in maintenance, property taxes, repairs, improvements and other home-owning expenses.

values and the likelihood of a prolonged real-estate recession in most of the country.

And like all other financial choices, how you go about taking money out of your house entails trade-offs. The sooner you start taking money out of your house, for example, the less money, in the very long run, you are likely to see. The flip side of that is that the longer you hold off tapping your nest egg, the more potential money you will have but the less time to spend it.

"I NEED THE MONEY NOW."

If like too many Americans, you have over-spent on your home and under-saved for your retirement, today's housing problems couldn't have come at a worse time. You are facing a market where you will be hard-pressed to sell your house, if you can find a buyer, at anything approaching the price you had hoped for just a few years ago. And if you are counting on your home equity to provide a significant portion of your retirement income, then you will need to prepare yourself for a markedly downscaled lifestyle.

For example, here's a couple in their middle sixties; let's call them Ted and Jane. Ted has just retired from his $80,000 a year sales job in southern California. He has no company pension, but he has built a respectable $250,000 balance in his 401(k). Jane has retired from her $40,000 a year teaching job. She gets a $1,000 a month pension and has $50,000 in a retirement fund.

They figure they will need about $6,000 a month to live the life they want in retirement. The couple expects to earn about $2,000 a month from their retirement funds and Jane's pension, and then another $2,700 a month from Social Security. Not bad, but still $1,300 short of their goal.

Unfortunately, Ted and Jane were counting on their modest house in the town of Covina, east of downtown Los Angeles, to make up the difference. Three years ago, a real-estate agent estimated the value of their house at $500,000, which the agent guessed could rise to as much as $600,000 by the time they'd be ready to sell. The agent guessed wrong. Today, Ted and Jane figure they'd be lucky to get $400,000 for the house.

They want to move to a new $250,000 place in Arizona, depositing the difference in a savings account or, better still, buying an annuity that will pay them a fixed income for the rest of their lives.

That might put Ted and Jane on a nice fairway somewhere, but it's hardly going to pay for the golf-and-tennis lifestyle that they dreamed of. The savings will earn them just an extra $500 or $600 a month—nice, but still well shy of their goal.

What options are open to them?

Sell and buy, cheaper. This is obvious, but it needn't be the end of the world. Ted and Jane could follow their original plan—sell in California and buy in Arizona—but settle for less in their new home. And it needn't be a lot less, either. Once again, it's a matter of needs versus wants.

For instance, in the Tucson area, which was a bargain for ex-pat West Coasters even before the bubble burst, the price spread between houses and comparable condominiums is just about perfect for people in Ted and Jane's predicament. If they buy for only about $150,000—choosing, say, a two-bedroom condo over a three-bedroom house—they will be able to pocket an additional $100,000.

This plan will double their rebate on their home—$200,000 after buying their new place instead of $100,000—and produce

$1,000 a month income, still shy of their goal but certainly within the ballpark.

Bonus: a condo is a lot better for an older couple than a house. At sixty-five or seventy, it may not make that much of a difference, but at eighty or eighty-five having someone else handling the day-to-day maintenance of your property is invaluable.

Remember: buying in today's market is buying for the long haul.

Sell and rent. Ted and Jane may end up getting a better deal if they don't buy right away. It's difficult to parachute into a new community and make a killer deal on a new house. They could move to Tucson and rent for a year or two. They may get to know the area well enough that they will find a house or a condo that they imagined but much cheaper than they thought. In the meantime, they can bank the entire $400,000 they'll get selling the California house. That will earn about $2,000 a month. Their new income will be high enough to offset their rental payments and still produce $1,000 a month of extra income.

Rent and rent. Ted and Jane could become landlords and rent out their California home while simultaneously renting in Tucson, where their rent will most likely be lower than what they are paid in Covina. Even with the rent differential, this plan won't produce a lot of extra income, but it does offer Ted and Jane some nice tax benefits. They will be able to use the depreciation on their California home to offset some of their income taxes. For example, if the building and improvements are worth $200,000, Ted and Jane would be able to write off about $7,200 a year against their rental income and, because they make less than $100,000 a year, the regular income as well.

Because they will be absentee landlords (not generally recommended), they will need to hire a local property manager to keep an eye on the place.

Sell on time. Similar to renting and renting, but with a big twist. Ted and Jane can have the regular income stream enjoyed by landlords with fewer hassles.

One of the big plusses of actually owning their home—as opposed to renting it from the bank with a mortgage—is that Ted and Jane have an asset that can actually make them money instead of just costing them money. There are a number of ways to do that, but a simple and potentially quite lucrative way to do that would be for them to become the lender when they sell their house. They could try offering a ten-year, interest-only loan as an inducement to buyers. The monthly payment for the buyer would be lower than a traditional amortized loan, and the term will be long enough, hopefully, for prices to start back up. After ten years, the buyer will need to take out a new loan and pay Ted and Jane their principal, or they could choose to roll over the loan with a new note and new interest rate. (This is just an example. You can structure any kind of loan you and your buyer want.)

There are three big advantages: Ted and Jane can ask and get a higher price for their property, they can set an interest rate higher than commercial lenders, and they can make a deal much easier and faster.

In this case, Ted and Jane might be able to get $425,000 or more for their place if they provide the financing. Taking a 10% down payment, they can give a 7% interest-only mortgage for ten years. The buyer will pay Ted and Jane $2,200 a month.

This strategy is not without pitfalls. The biggest risk, of course, is that Ted and Jane's buyer will default on the loan. That would cost them about six months of payments, but they would end up with the house, which they could then sell again. To Ted and Jane's favor, however, even a marginal borrower would not be as risky in this case as during the sub-prime debacle. First, Ted and Jane's buyer won't be facing an unmanageable interest-rate reset, and if the buyer does get in trouble, Ted and Jane have a lot more flexibility than commercial lenders in dealing with the problem.

More caveats: Ted and Jane will need a real-estate attorney to set this up for them (including seeing that they have mortgage insurance to cover the downside) and a bank or lending company to handle the payments (new "peer-to-peer" lenders are doing this sort of thing; see *http://www.virginmoneyus.com*).

"I'LL NEED THE MONEY LATER."

The biggest problem about retirement today is that people live too long.

Yes, it *does* beat the alternative, but with so many retirees now living well into their eighties and beyond, they are straining the retirement system. And not just Social Security and Medicare. The real strain is on private savings. People, even prudent people who were careful and built up sizeable nest eggs, are simply outliving their own retirement plans.

Imagine your retirement in two phases. The first begins in your sixties. That's the long vacation that most of us dream about at the end of a lifetime of labor—no work, no boss, lots of travel, fishing, golf, tennis, no snow to shovel, no kids to raise but lots of grandchildren to spoil, doing what you want when you want and how you want. It's costly, but generally manageable, even for people who haven't saved as much as they might have.

It's the second retirement that wallops you and your finances. It starts later, when age finally takes a firm hold of you. You're not as active. Your health declines. Eventually, you may need daily help, either at home or in an assisted-living facility. It's difficult and it's hugely expensive, with a bill of $180,000 for the average two-and-a-half-year nursing-home stay. Full-time in-home care can cost that much in a year. (You can count on those expenses to double by the time the vanguard of Boomers hit their eighties.)

Here's where your biggest asset can come in.

One of the best ways to weather the financial storm at the end of life is a reverse mortgage. Reverse mortgages are ridiculously expensive and complicated, but they are one of the very few ways that home owners can use a significant portion of the equity they have in their primary residences without selling or moving or facing new drains on their cash flow. Reverse mortgages are not perfect—they cost a lot of money—but they are one practical solution to a horrendous financial and social problem that will grow worse as the Baby Boomers slip further into old age.

Think of a reverse mortgage as your last line of financial defense. If Ted and Jane, for instance, chose to stay in their California home and take out a reverse mortgage, they could receive almost $1,100 a month right away or wait ten years and receive nearly $1,400 a month. Other reverse mortgage options include open lines of credit that grow over time but can be tapped when needed, giving Ted and Jane a comfortable cushion when they may really need it in fifteen or twenty years.

Here are the basics:

- A reverse mortgage is *a loan that you don't have to pay back until you sell your house.* There are no monthly or periodic payments by the borrower to the lender, only a payback when you sell, move out or pass away. Be aware that most reverse mortgages carry adjustable rates that are one or two percentage points higher than comparable "forward" or traditional mortgage rates—which is part of the reason they end up being so expensive.

- There are three basic types of reverse mortgages but the *most popular are federally insured Home Equity Conversion Mortgages (HECM),* backed by the U.S. Department of Housing and Urban Development but offered through private lenders and banks under government guidelines. These have lending limits that vary according to the location of a home. In addition to HECMs, there are *"proprietary" reverse mortgages,* which are private loans backed by the companies and banks that offer them. These generally have higher fees but also higher loan limits than government-backed mortgages. One popular proprietary loan is Fannie Mae's "Home Keeper" reverse mortgage. Finally, there are state- or local-government sponsored *"public-sector" reverse mortgage loans* that are made for specific purposes such as home repairs or property-tax deferral, usually, though not always, to low or moderate income households.

- Generally, *the more valuable your home is and the older you are, the more you can borrow.* HECM and Home Keeper loans have similar requirements. They are available for retirement-age home owners who live in their homes. There are no credit requirements, but the loan limit is based on the age of the youngest borrower if, for instance, a husband and wife own the house jointly (all borrowers must be at least sixty-two), interest rates and the appraised value of the property. Any borrower of a federally backed loan must visit a HUD-approved mortgage counselor, who will explain the various loan options and figure the long-term loan expenses *(http://www.hud.gov/offices/hsg/sfh/hecm/hecmhome.cfm).*

- *Interest is charged only as funds are withdrawn.* Reverse mortgage loans can be made in lump sums, as monthly payments from the lender to the borrower, open lines of credit or some combination of the three. If you set up an HECM line of credit and don't tap it right away, the amount available will increase over the years.

- HECM loans are *available for most residential properties*— single-family homes, one- to four-unit buildings, condominiums, cooperative apartments or manufactured homes. A variant on the Home Keeper loan can be used to buy a new home.

- There's nothing free about reverse mortgages. They are *very expensive to set up,* although you aren't required to pay the expenses out of pocket. For a typical HECM, fees can be folded into the loan amount, but they are still high—an origination fee equal to 2% of the loan value, plus a 2% insurance fee based on the difference between the loan balance and value of the house, plus all the other closing costs that come with a new mortgage. Fees of $12,000 to $15,000

ALTERNATIVES TO A REVERSE MORTGAGE

Besides the traditional reverse mortgage, there are other ways to take money out of your house or to transfer it to your children:

Sale-leaseback. Sell your home to the kids but continue to live in it, paying a fair-market rent.

Home equity line of credit. You can still open a HELOC and use it as part of your emergency fund. Unlike a reverse mortgage, however, you will need to pay back whatever money you take out, as with any other type of traditional loan.

Programs that help with real estate taxes, repairs. Most state governments have programs that provide special purpose loans to seniors to pay property taxes or make home repairs or improvements. Like reverse mortgages, these types of loans are not repaid until the borrower moves, sells or dies. To find out what's available, go first to: *http://www.aarp.org/money/ revmort/revmort_choices/*.

on a house worth $200,000 would not be unusual. Then get ready for another ½% insurance fee every year and a $30 or so monthly servicing fee.

• And you have to pay it back. When you sell, move out or pass away, *the reverse mortgage loan must be paid with all the accumulated interest.* That can be a substantial sum, more than enough to eat up all the value of a modest house. Fortunately, however, all that expensive mortgage insurance on an HECM loan assures that the borrower, or the borrower's estate, won't be hit with a bill if the value of the house when it's finally sold is less than the loan balance.

It's not easy to figure how much money you can borrow with a reverse mortgage. As I said earlier, the formula is based on a combination of your age, prevailing interest rates, the

WHAT *NOT* TO DO WITH A REVERSE MORTGAGE

Pay fees up front. Loan fees should be included in the loan balance and paid when the loan is settled. Don't let any lender talk you into taking a lump sum and paying fees when you get the loan. That's a scam.

Pay off a traditional mortgage. Many borrowers do, and it's a much-touted benefit of reverse mortgages. But it's best not to. The long-term payoff of a reverse mortgage will cost far more than paying off what's left on your existing balance. If you have enough savings, it's better to use that and pay off the existing mortgage, and then take out a reverse mortgage.

Invest in the market. Don't try to beat the stock market or make any other investment with your reverse mortgage payout. You're not likely to come out ahead—the interest rate and fees are just too high. If you don't need the loan money right away, leave it where it is—in your house—until you do. If you don't tap the loan principal, the available balance actually goes up as you get older.

Put in a hot tub. Many elderly home owners get talked into paying for consumer goods or unneeded home improvements with their reverse mortgage payments. Don't. If you want to buy something other than a necessity, shop skeptically.

Buy an annuity. A reverse mortgage functions much like an annuity, so you don't need to use your mortgage-loan money to buy another one. Furthermore, the costs of an annuity plus a reverse mortgage are certain to be greater than the cost of just a reverse mortgage alone.

property itself and where it is. The AARP maintains a good site with reverse mortgage information including a useful online calculator *(http://www.aarp.org/money/revmort)* developed by NETirement.com. It's the easiest way to get a ballpark estimate on what you can get.

Let's look at how some people might use reverse mortgages to help pay for their retirements:

Fred and Ethel, an eighty-two-year-old man and his seventy-eight-year-old wife, live in a $500,000 house in Chicago. Fred's still in pretty good shape—no major physical or mental problems—but he is, as he frequently points out, "getting up there."

Fred's concerned about how well Ethel will be able to live after he's gone, so he's exploring a reverse mortgage as a retirement supplement. If the couple opened an HECM-style mortgage now, they would be able to choose, as can all borrowers, among an immediate lump sum payment, a monthly advance, or an open-ended line of credit that will grow every year. (The amount available is based on Ethel's expected life span, by the way, because she is the younger of the two.)

Because money isn't a big issue for the couple, their wisest move would be to take out the loan now but wait and let the available-funds balance grow until Ethel needs to tap it. If she waits ten years, the money available will grow by an additional $100,000.

What if you need some money right away? A reverse mortgage can help, but it's probably not the best way to go if you are just starting your retirement.

Let's look at another scenario: Marc and Jennifer, both sixty-two years old, are typical "house poor" soon-to-retire own-

FRED AND ETHEL'S REVERSE MORTGAGE OPTIONS	
	HECM
Single lump sum	$189,942
Monthly payment	$1,255
Line of credit (grows 4.31%/year)	$189,942
5 years	$235,592
10 years	$289,738

ers with more home than savings. They had planned on retiring at sixty-two, selling their house in the inland part of the San Diego area, pocketing some dough and moving to a condo closer to the ocean. The house seemed rather modest to them when they bought it thirty years ago, but its value ballooned with the rest of California real estate, reaching an estimated value of $1 million during the bubble. Today, if they could find a buyer, they'd consider themselves lucky if they could get $750,000.

They had planned to move into a new place and use whatever money was left over to buy an annuity. They had counted on a nest egg of about $400,000—enough to generate about $2,300 a month until they both die. Today, condos are a steal in hard-hit San Diego, but Marc and Jennifer don't want to lose so much appreciation on their existing home. They want to hold off for a while on their plan to move. They decide Jennifer will go ahead and retire while Marc will work for another couple of years. They commit to their house for another ten years, by which time, they hope, prices will be back to bubble-era levels.

They choose to take out a reverse mortgage, however, as a safety net in case the economy gets worse. Their goal is to let the balance grow and dip into it from time to time only for repairs and other big-ticket items.

MARC AND JENNIFER'S REVERSE MORTGAGE OPTIONS	
	HECM
Single lump sum	$204,176
Monthly payment	$1,071
Line of credit (grows 3.69%/year)	$204,176
5 years	$244,743
10 years	$293,370

LUCY'S REVERSE MORTGAGE OPTIONS

	HECM
Single lump sum	$121,848
Monthly payment	$702
Line of credit (grows 4.31%/year)	$121,848
5 years	$150,490
10 years	$185,866

Finally, here's a scenario on a $200,000 house in Nashville owned by a single seventy-year-old woman, Lucy. She has Social Security, a modest pension from her late husband's job and dwindling savings. She would like to boost her income, but she's also concerned about having enough money for her eighties, when she may need more help tending to her day-to-day activities.

One thing clear from these scenarios is that the amount of money available to borrowers varies greatly. Something equally noticeable is the paltry amount of money that you can get— just $204,000 on a $750,000 house!

Why? Because long-term mortgages are expensive. And this is a *reverse* mortgage; the loan balance increases year after year as you pile on more interest and then owe interest on the interest.

Fortunately, it's usually a borrower's estate—not the borrower himself or herself—that pays the final bills. And in the case of reverse mortgages, the amount that the borrower must pay back can't exceed the value of the sold house. (Among all those hefty fees the borrower paid was an insurance premium to compensate the lender if the value of the house doesn't cover the value of the loan balance.)

That said, there is one sure way to maximize the income of a reverse mortgage. Don't use it. Not until you need it, that is. There are two good reasons for that: First, a reverse mortgage is more valuable the later you borrow the money. Second, a reverse mortgage grows exponentially more expensive the earlier you use it.

To better understand this, let's look at a couple more charts, prepared for this book with a reverse-mortgage amortizing calculator developed by Karl Ebert of KJE Computer Solutions in Minneapolis. It's available for use free at *http://www.dinkytown.net*.

Here's the twenty-year cost of a 7.5% HECM loan on Lucy's Nashville house if she takes a lump-sum payout of $121,848:

Year	Advance	Interest	Balance
A 20-YEAR REVERSE MORTGAGE ON A MODEST HOUSE IN NASHVILLE			
	$121,848		$121,848
1	$0	$9,139	$130,987
2	$0	$9,824	$140,811
3	$0	$10,561	$151,371
4	$0	$11,353	$162,724
5	$0	$12,204	$174,929
6	$0	$13,120	$188,048
7	$0	$14,104	$202,152
8	$0	$15,161	$217,313
9	$0	$16,298	$233,612
10	$0	$17,521	$251,133
11	$0	$18,835	$269,968
12	$0	$20,248	$290,215
13	$0	$21,766	$311,981
14	$0	$23,399	$335,380
15	$0	$25,153	$360,533
16	$0	$27,040	$387,573
17	$0	$29,068	$416,641
18	$0	$31,248	$447,889
19	$0	$33,592	$481,481
20	**$0**	**$36,111**	**$517,592**

That's a lot of money. Who knows what a $200,000 house in Nashville will be worth in twenty years—$500,000 is probably not out of the realm of possibility if the housing market resumes its traditional trajectory—but it's daunting, to say the least, to see the balance rise so high so fast. (Really daunting: the balance will reach more than $1 million if Lucy lives to 100.)

All in all, taking a lump sum is not the smartest way to tap the built-up equity. There is a better, less expensive way for Lucy. She should take only monthly payments. She could take $702 a month ($8,424 a year) for as long as she lives in her house and end up owing much less than if she had taken a lump sum. If she lives to ninety, Lucy or her estate will end up

	MONTHLY ADVANCES ON A REVERSE MORTGAGE		
Year	Advance	Interest	Balance
Start	$0		$0
1	$8,424	$338	$8,762
2	$8,424	$996	$18,182
3	$8,424	$1,702	$28,308
4	$8,424	$2,462	$39,194
5	$8,424	$3,278	$50,896
6	$8,424	$4,156	$63,475
7	$8,424	$5,099	$76,998
8	$8,424	$6,113	$91,536
9	$8,424	$7,204	$107,163
10	$8,424	$8,376	$123,963
11	$8,424	$9,636	$142,023
12	$8,424	$10,990	$161,437
13	$8,424	$12,446	$182,307
14	$8,424	$14,011	$204,743
15	$8,424	$15,694	$228,861
16	$8,424	$17,503	$254,788
17	$8,424	$19,448	$282,659
18	$8,424	$21,538	$312,621
19	$8,424	$23,785	$344,830
20	$8,424	$26,201	$379,455

owing $380,000—still a lot of money, to be sure, but much less than if she had started with a lump sum.

Finally, Lucy could maximize her reverse mortgage loan if she can afford to wait until very late to tap it—until, for example, she needs constant nursing care at age eighty-seven.

In the seventeen years between the time she opens the loan and when she finally borrows from it, the available money would grow from $122,000 to $244,500, enough to provide Lucy with more than $24,000 a year for the next decade. If Lucy moves permanently to a nursing home, she or her family would be required to sell the house a year after moving out, but if she stays in the house, she could take lower payments and continue to live in her home indefinitely.

"I WANT TO LEAVE SOMETHING TO THE CHILDREN."

Fortunately, not everyone needs to get money out of their home. For some, their house is a component of their wealth—but not something that has to be sold or borrowed against. Those people are the most likely to build the most wealth in their homes—and use it to benefit posterity.

Without a doubt, home owners accumulate more wealth and leave larger estates than non-owners, setting up later generations for increased financial security and all of the benefits that come with it.

In all but the wealthiest of families, the house remains the biggest single component of family net worth and a huge factor in its transfer of wealth between generations. Indeed, the great home-owning wealth-building machine usually ends up benefiting children far more than it does the parents who bought the house. That's because the parents most likely ended up paying far more for their house than its actual value. Not so for the kids. They get handed a sizeable bit of property, already bought and paid for.

Therefore, the goal for any transfer of assets to your heirs is to maximize the value of the bequest while minimizing the taxes that might be paid on it. In leaving a house to your children or grandchildren, you will generally want to transfer at the current value of the property but remain within the limits of tax-free giving from one generation to the next. For families living in average priced homes, there are no obstacles to simply passing a house on along with the other family possessions. House values outside the nation's most expensive neighborhoods fall well below the lower limits for estate taxes.

For owners of more expensive homes, though, here's the very best, most tax-efficient thing you can do: die in 2010. That's because for 2010 only, estate taxes will disappear completely.

It's been nearly a decade since Congress started easing away from estate taxes by raising the wealth threshold where the tax kicks in—up from a 55% tax rate on estates worth more than $675,000 in 2001 to the 2009 rate of 45% on anything above $3.5 million. They are eliminated completely in 2010, but then reappear in 2011. (These numbers apply to individuals; husbands and wives can each pass along amounts up to the exemption threshold.) It is widely believed, however, that Congress will institute new benchmarks before the old rule is reinstituted.

Still, regardless of what you may hear or read about "death taxes" or families forced to liquidate their treasures in order to pay estate taxes to the U.S. Treasury, most of the talk is hokum. Only a handful of American families at the very tip of the economic pyramid have any tax bills when it comes to passing Mom and Dad's house to Junior and Sissy—and they have legions of expensive lawyers who work the system to its limits to minimize the government's tax bite.

To be sure, some home owners on the expensive coasts were unprepared for the price increases of the modest homes they bought in the 1950s and '60s and found themselves fast approaching estate-tax territory. Today a middle-class California family's suburban tract home can easily be worth $1 million or more. Likewise, in the pricier zip codes of New York,

ESTATE TAXES		
Year	Exclusion	Tax rate
2001	$675,000	55%
2002	$1,000,000	50%
2003	$1,000,000	49%
2004	$1,500,000	48%
2005	$1,500,000	47%
2006	$2,000,000	46%
2007	$2,000,000	45%
2008	$2,000,000	45%
2009	$3,500,000	45%
2010	repealed	0%
2011	$1,000,000	55%

family-sized condos or co-ops sell for more than $2 million. We're not talking the super-wealthy here, just your average house-rich millionaires next door. And they *could* face IRS issues if the estate-tax exemptions fall back to just $1 million.

Fortunately, the government that writes laws to take money away also writes laws to give it back. Even if Congress lets the lower limits stay at the $1 million mark, it's still possible to avoid the big tax bite. Here are some ways:

Stay where you are. If you want to remain in your home, and your total estate, including the house, is below whatever the tax-exemption threshold may be at the time, your children can simply take over the property at its "stepped up" value (fair-market value) at the time of your death. And the kids are free to move in or sell it. There's no estate tax, no capital gains tax on the transfer of the house, and no income tax if they sell it.

Give the house away. Here you are using the $1 million gift-tax exemption—which says you can pass along that much money in your lifetime tax free. But this gets complicated.

If you are moving out of your home, you can give the property to your child today. However, you will probably have to dip into your $1 million gift-tax exemption as well as the estate-tax exemption. Here's how it works.

First, offset the amount of the gift by using your $12,000 annual gift-tax exclusion. Remember, it's $12,000 per donor, so if you and your husband each make a gift to both your son and his wife, you can offset $48,000 of the home's value. Then, as long as the net figure is less than $1 million, you won't owe any gift taxes.

Still, there are two problems with this that you should be aware of: First, if your son ever sells the property, his "cost basis" will be what you paid for the house way back when. That mean's he'll probably owe the IRS a sizeable piece of the action at the time of sale. Second, you've taken out a substantial portion of estate-tax exemption—which could be a problem if you have other assets you want to pass along.

Sell it for a pittance. This can get dicey. Sell for a bargain price to any Joe or Jane who drops by your open house, and the IRS doesn't care. Give Junior or Sissy a big price break, however, and the IRS will say you are making a gift equal to the difference between the fair-market value of the house and the sale price.

If your house is worth $600,000 and you sell it to your daughter for $350,000, the IRS will say that you made a gift of $250,000. That's going to eat up some of your lifetime gift-tax exemption, but it will greatly reduce your daughter's cost basis on the home.

Sell it over time. Better than a fire-sale price is an installment sale for full market value. Don't try this without a good lawyer and accountant, but if you do it right, you can transfer the house to your son at full value with very little money actually changing hands. Just make gifts every year that roughly equal the mortgage payments. Your son will get a nifty bonus tax deduction. And you can funnel even more money to him by renting your house from him without running afoul of the tax laws.

Set up an A-B trust. This avoids a typical problem among

GIVE IT AWAY

If the house isn't a huge portion of your net worth, income isn't a big issue, or your children aren't interested in taking it over, you can give your home to charity. Families with more than one house—whether a vacation home or rental property—often end up donating one. Any charitable organization will help you set up your donation, but do have your own lawyer set up the deal. Here are some ways to donate your home:

A simple gift. The property is removed from your taxable estate, and you receive a charitable tax deduction equal to the appraised value of the property. The charity will take over the donated property and most likely sell it.

Charitable trust. The most common strategy used in the donation of houses is called a charitable remainder trust. You transfer ownership of the house to a trust, which then sells the house and holds the sale proceeds. You and your spouse can use the trust income, usually, until both of you are dead. Then the trust passes to the charity. You receive a charitable tax deduction for a portion of the property's value.

Retained life estate. You give the house away, but you and your spouse continue to live in it for life. The charity takes over the house when you die and sells it. You receive a charitable tax deduction when you donate the house for a portion of the property's value.

Sell for less than fair-market value. You sell a property to a charity for less than its appraised value. You receive a tax deduction for the difference. The charity resells the property for full value.

Standard bequest. Unlike a gift, a bequest is donated from your will, and your estate will be reduced by the size of the donation.

well-to-do couples that arises when one spouse dies and leaves everything to the surviving spouse. When the now single surviving spouse eventually passes away, she's allowed to pass along only half of what she and her husband could have left together. With an A-B trust, the husband and wife put their halves of the family wealth into trusts that benefit the surviving spouse but names the children as final beneficiaries.

Set up a qualified personal residence trust. You can make an IRS-approved gift of your home while still living in it with a qualified personal residence trust (QPRT). This is used mainly by the very wealthy transferring valuable properties: Think of passing along the $5 million condo in Palm Beach to your daughters. Daddy and Mumsie put the place in an irrevocable trust for several years, while they live in it. Through a complex IRS calculation based on interest rates, the length of the trust and their ages, the IRS values their rights to live in the house at, say, $3 million. When the trust is up after the stipulated number of years, the parents can continue living there by paying their daughters rent, further reducing the size of their estates. One big catch: Make sure you're in good health. If you die before the term of the trust expires, the full date-of-death value of the house is included in your taxable estate and your heirs receive no estate-tax benefit.

CHAPTER 8

THE
PURSUIT
OF
HAPPINESS

The best time to buy a home is always five years ago.

— RAY BROWN

As I said at the beginning, this book is about your dreams and the money you will need to achieve them. That you picked up this book from all the others in the store suggests that at least one of your dreams is to own your own home.

That's a good one. And it's a dream shared by millions of other Americans. We are a nation with the home-owning gene deeply embedded in our DNA. Our government's commitment to widespread home ownership and its efforts to encourage home owning—from mortgage guarantees to tax breaks—are unique among advanced nations. Home owning and home life are mainstays of our mass-media culture—from family sitcoms and home-makeover TV shows to cutting-edge fashion and design magazines. We revere and make pilgrimages to the preserved homes of our founding fathers and even of our rock-and-roll stars.

But there are plenty of other good dreams out there, too, that need attention and money. Run for president. Open a business. Become an organic farmer. Maybe you want to go to Harvard. Or maybe you want to own your own software company. Or maybe you want to drop out of Harvard to start your own software company.

And that's the real American dream—that you can aspire to and pursue whatever dream or dreams you want. For too many Americans, however, the dream of home owning has gotten in the way of their other dreams. Home ownership has become all-consuming, overwhelming even, as families must defer or abandon other dreams just to meet a house's unrelenting demands for more and more money.

For centuries, rich, middle-class and poor Americans have shared at least two life goals: First, we want to build for ourselves a comfortable life that satisfies us materially and spiritually. Second, we want to provide for our children the opportunities to build for themselves lives that further enhance the blessings of our diligence and good fortune.

For all of our recorded history, the principal avenue for achieving these goals has been the ownership of property. Property for most early European-Americans meant a farm or a shop, where the family home and the family business were one in the same. But since World War II, property ownership has meant owning your own home.

Today, that means of pursuing happiness faces its greatest test. The notion that a home is the safest repository of your money and a sure path to wealth has been discredited. Gene Epstein, a writer for *Barron's,* the financial news magazine, did some research on the last housing bubble in the United States and came up with the sobering, scary conclusion: adjusting for inflation, Gene found that house prices last peaked in 1979, fell for five years, and then slowly recovered for the next eleven years. It took sixteen years for the boom-bust cycle to play through.

So where will you be in 2022?

AN EVOLVING DREAM

There were always wealthy people who had grand town houses or country mansions, but few of us today can imagine the miserable living conditions of most of our forefathers and foremothers. Cows and horses probably had more space in their barn stalls than most people enjoyed in their houses. In eighteenth-century New England, for instance, even a prosperous farmer's household might include father and mother, children, servants and perhaps a boarder or two in a space smaller than a modern one-bedroom apartment. In the cities where building lots were small, a shopkeeper's family would feel lucky if they had more than one room above the store.

With industrialization and commercialized agriculture came houses that, for the very wealthy, made grand statements about the owner's prosperity and power.

Humble farms and shops thrived, leading families still had their big homes and professionals had their offices on the parlor floors. But the gritty mill towns of the North were dominated, like feudal baronies, by the mine or factory and its owner's lavish, showplace palace. The owner's home became a symbol of the benefits of industry and economic freedom— all the more pointed because the mansion could be seen from the squalid, overpriced slum housing the owner rented to his workers.

Meanwhile in the South, the owner commanded his vast land holdings from a columned, fairy-tale manor house. From his portico, the owner could survey all his wealth, which included the workers themselves as well as the fields where they labored and the crude shanties where they slept.

Over the one hundred years after the Civil War, there emerged a new sense and new form of property ownership. Life and labor divorced. The concept of a house separate from the workplace or the family's principal means of income began to drift down the economic ladder. Like the factory owners, the very rich had long been able to afford to live away from their work. Eventually, that became an option for the middle and working classes, too.

The American house became much more than an adjunct to the family business, more that just a place to sleep, eat and raise children. The house became a *home,* a refuge from the world and a reward for work, thrift, clean living and other virtues. The home became something more and more people aspired to own.

In short, the home became the physical manifestation of the American dream. In 1900, less than 20% of the population owned single-family homes that weren't farmhouses. Just sixty years later, more than 60% of the country would own their homes, most far, far away from their offices, shops or factories in the vast suburban tracks made possible by cheap gasoline and the interstate highway system.

The dream came first to the well-to-do of the professional and business classes. Streetcars made it possible for Father to work Downtown while Mother oversaw the staff and the children in the family's jaunty Uptown Italiante or grand Garden District Queen Anne. Railroads pushed the home front even farther—out to the suburbs, where the haute bourgeoisie raised Colonial Revivals and Tudors where the upper crust had built their Neoclassical and Beaux Arts mansions a generation before.

And after the Depression and World War II, the automobile and a new era of democratic prosperity offered the dream to millions and millions of middle- and working-class families, who filled the countryside with Cape Cods and Split Levels.

The post-war workers didn't quite move up to the Big House, but they did move into an 800-square-foot, two-bedroom, one-bath single-story Everyman's castle on a one-sixth-of-an-acre lot.

Before the war, there were rather few home mortgages, at least the kind that we know today. Early in the century, farmers had mortgages that they borrowed and then paid off year after year, but the vast majority of home owners saved *before* they bought and paid cash for their houses. Later, buyers who put down 40% or 50% of the house price could get five-year or ten-year mortgages. In the Depression, the government began insuring very long-term mortgages, and buyers started making twenty- and thirty-year commitments, usually, but not always, with 20% down payments.

In 1949, a family moving from New York City to the suburbanizing bean fields of Long Island could buy a brand-new Levittown "Ranch" for just $7,990. Veterans paid nothing down and had a monthly payment of about $72. That was a stretch to be sure, but just a few dollars more than the $65 a month rent that Levitt & Sons charged for the 1947 models.

The greatest land rush in U.S. history was on, and the nation was transformed in less than a generation. From 1940 to 1960, home ownership in the United States jumped from 15 million households to 33 million, or 62% of the country. At the top of the most recent housing bubble, 70 million owners occupied their own homes, about 69%.

And over time, that modest 800-square-footer supersized. Today, the average new home is a 2,300-square-foot, two-story palace with a 300-square-foot kitchen, a family room and a living room, at least three bedrooms, two-and-a-half baths, central air-conditioning and a two-car garage. (Food for thought: Maybe the workers *have* made it to the Big House. Today's average new home is just 300 square feet smaller than the living area of George and Martha Washington's main house at Mount Vernon.)

In the 1970s, as the World War II generation moved toward retirement and their children grew into their own prime home-buying years, yet another change in the idea of property ownership took hold. The American dream became Americans' savings accounts.

Before the '70s, it was rare to see home owning touted for its financial benefits. Quite the opposite. In the forty years before World War II, home prices actually declined. One popular 1947 book, *How to Buy or Build a Home of Your Own: A*

Complete Guide to Home Ownership, took the old lesson to heart and pointedly informed readers that they shouldn't expect their new home to make them rich. "Do not buy your home ... under the misconception that real property in the long run always increases in value. Take it for granted, instead, that your house will tend to decline in value as time goes on."

But what happened in the '70s was the convergence of historically high inflation, widespread home ownership among a generation on the verge of retirement, and a tsunami of Baby Boomers shopping for their first homes. Inflation pushed up the value of all hard assets, creating the appearance of an enormous windfall for the owners who saw their post-war houses balloon in value. For owners raised amid the depravations of the Great Depression, the inflation-fueled home prices went far beyond their experiences and expectations. They grew rich just sitting there!

On the day Richard Nixon was sworn in as president in 1969, the average home in the country was worth $23,700; twelve years later, when Ronald Reagan took office, that average house was worth $78,300. Now, *that* was a bubble! That was an increase of 230% in just twelve years, and the fastest, biggest percentage run-up since World War II.

Talk about American dreams. The Boomers bought into a market that looked like it could only go up. The family home was no longer just a symbol of prosperity. It was prosperity itself.

It played that role for three more decades. But today, it's a different story.

WHAT EVERY HOME OWNER NEEDS TO KNOW

For the next few years, Americans will be grappling with the problem of *home,* redefining where the floor beneath our feet now fits in our democratic-free enterprise scheme of things. Indeed, we, each of us, will be rethinking where our homes fit in our own personal schemes, whether we will again be able to look on our houses as the foundations of our family wealth and financial security.

Among the lessons of the burst bubble:

- Home values don't always go up. Diversify your investments to include a variety of assets.

- For 99% of us, home buying is and will remain borrowing. Never borrow more than you can pay.

- Rising home values cover a multitude of mistakes; sinking values uncover them. Some days, there are no buyers and no lenders.

As all this plays out, other lessons are certain to come to you. Until then, all you can do is approach home buying and home owning sensibly and prudently. A house is a huge commitment of money, time and self. Be smart about it.

Let's wrap this up. Here are the big points—twenty of them—that have been covered throughout the book. They're the essence of what every home buyer and home owner needs to know to successfully manage his or her biggest asset:

1. **A house is a big expense.** But it's not necessarily a great investment. A house doesn't make money. It costs money. It's not cash, not stocks, not bonds, not anything at all that acts like a typical investment. As with any other hard asset, unless you are selling, the only way you can take cash out of your home is to borrow against it. And that means you, not the house, will be paying the bills.

2. **The investment returns are mediocre.** From the 1980s through the most recent real-estate bubble, the investment return of owner-occupied residential properties has averaged just a percentage point or so above inflation—far, far below the returns for stocks. As the nation works its

way through the post-boom real-estate depression, returns for existing home owners are most likely to lag well behind inflation.

3. **The tax benefits of home buying are exaggerated.** The mortgage-interest deduction and the big capital-gain exclusion do very little for the vast majority of home owners. The interest deduction's value is worth only the difference between the mortgage interest you pay and the value of the "standard deduction" available to all taxpayers. And the definition of what constitutes a capital gain for a home seller is so narrow that it excludes most of the costs of owning.

4. **Buy versus rent is the wrong question.** In the very long run, home buyers almost always end up better off financially than renters. But the bigger issue isn't whether to rent or buy; it's *how much* to buy. Spend less money on your house, and you will have more money to spend on more productive investments. Every dollar you spend buying and owning a house is a dollar that is not going into your business, your 401(k), your Roth IRA, your college-savings fund or any other investment.

5. **It's a buyers' market.** The United States is on the back side of the tremendous price run-ups in the 2000–2006 era. This is a down cycle that will see overall values fall 25% or more from their bubble-era highs. There will be specific metropolitan areas and specific neighborhoods and communities that will defy the trend. But overall, prices are falling and will continue to fall or stay flat for the foreseeable future. Including the effects of inflation, home prices may not recover their bubble-era highs until the 2020s.

6. **As in all markets, this one will have winners and losers.** The depressed housing market will most benefit first-time home buyers and mid-cycle, move-up buyers with enough cash or other assets to buy without selling their current

homes. If you have a secure job, ample savings and good credit, you are in a position to acquire your dream home at a huge discount. Suffering the greatest problems in this market will be early-cycle owners who bought their houses during the bubble and late-cycle owners who have counted on their homes to pay for a significant portion of their retirement needs.

7. **Buyer-owners should focus on their mortgages.** There's no such thing as "good" debt. A mortgage might qualify as better debt than a credit card, but it's still a debt and it's still the most expensive part of buying a home. The best way to manage your biggest asset is to manage your biggest debt. Home buyers should be especially wary of exotic interest-only home-purchase loans or "negative amortization" mortgages.

8. **Make sure your mortgage fits your life.** Whether you get a fixed-rate mortgage or an adjustable-rate mortgage (ARM) should depend solely on how long you plan to hold on to the house. If you plan to move in a few years, then an ARM is best. If you are in for the long haul, then a fixed-rate mortgage will be more manageable. Never take out an ARM just because the payment is lower and you can buy a more expensive house.

9. **Pay off your first mortgage quickly.** Whether fixed or adjustable, a good mortgage is a paid mortgage. The quicker you pay it, the cheaper the overall cost of buying your house will be and the sooner you'll be free to make other acquisitions or to make more productive investments. In a market in which you can't anticipate significant value appreciation, the only way you will build your ownership interest in your home is to pay down the mortgage balance.

10. **Borrow equity wisely.** Borrowing against your home equity is pawning your house. Be careful out there. Refinance your first mortgage or take out a home-equity loan only if

it benefits you in both the short and long terms. Merely swapping a high monthly payment for a smaller one will do you no good if at the same time you commit to many more years of payments. "Cash-out" refinancing that stretches out consumer debt for thirty years or is used to buy consumer goods is a waste of money if it merely exchanges high-interest revolving credit with lower-interest but longer-term mortgage credit.

11. **Use equity borrowing to your advantage.** If you use home equity to manage other expenses, borrow with only short-term home-equity loans or lines of credit. Loans secured by your home equity will always carry lower interest rates than consumer loans, so disciplined use of home-equity borrowing can significantly reduce your interest charges elsewhere. And home-equity lines of credit can play an important part in your family's emergency planning—but only as a supplement for savings, not as a substitute.

12. **Buying today is buying for the long haul.** In this market, you won't be able to trade your way up to Beverly Hills by buying and selling every five years or so. There won't be enough price appreciation to support that kind of activity, and you probably won't acquire enough equity in just five years to make a dent in the price of a new house. So, if you are shopping in this marked-down market, be sure the place you're buying is a place you will be comfortable staying in for ten or fifteen years. Likewise, if your marriage isn't that strong or you think you may want to make a job-related move in a couple of years, don't buy. Keep renting.

13. **Think and act like a pro.** Not like an amateur. Whether you are buying, living in or selling a home, you should operate in a financially prudent manner. You are not a speculator. You're a highly leveraged borrower who hopes one day to own your own home. The best way to get there is to make sure that you don't overpay for your home to begin

with, that you negotiate a price 30% or more below the bubble-era value of the house, and that you keep your owning expenses as low as possible for as long as you hold on to the property.

14. **Determine the real value and stick to it.** Sales comps are not sufficient to determine the value of a home. They merely tell you what amateur buyers are paying for similar properties. Appraisers and professional property investors also take into consideration the replacement value of a house and, more important for a home buyer, the rental value. You should, too. If the potential rental income for a property is not sufficient to cover the mortgage and other expenses, then the price is too high. If you are buying, negotiate the seller down or look elsewhere.

15. **Don't sell unless you have to.** Sellers have no negotiating clout in this market. Owners without a lot of cash savings should plan to spend many more years in the house they currently own. Sell only if you must move for health, job or pressing financial issues. If you must sell, then sell. Don't beat around the bush. Hire a good agent, set a reasonable, saleable price *for this market,* and negotiate with the first solid buyer who comes along with an offer in the right ballpark.

16. **Watch the remodeling.** If you are staying in your house, be extra prudent with your remodeling. Renovate for your *needs.* Extravagant renovating rarely pays for itself, even in booming real-estate markets, and is a sure money loser in this one. Look first to reallocate existing space within your house before you expand. Avoid long-term borrowing; pay cash or take out only short-term loans.

17. **Save by the hour.** Energy conservation is good personal finance and good global policy. Make repairs, renovations or replace existing appliances and systems with the goal of

reducing your energy consumption and minimizing the environmental impact of your house. You'll do well and good. There are ample government and energy-company programs that help home owners cut their costs.

18. **Decide what you want your house to be.** Make plans for your home before you are too old to make the right plans. There will come a time when you decide whether to keep your house or move. You can sell it, you can donate it, you can pass it along to your children, but each requires a different set of decisions. Be careful, if you plan to sell and move, today's declining values will hit you hard.

19. **You *can* treat it like a savings account.** As you age and draw down your retirement savings, your home can serve as your asset of last resort. If you live into your eighties, you may well need to tap the equity in your home to live. This can be done a number of ways, but one of the easiest for you and your heirs is a reverse mortgage. Set it up early, but don't draw on it until later.

20. **Build a legacy.** Your family's home is not the means to financial security, it's the result.

Throughout this book, I have tried to separate the emotions of home owning from the finances. Money is essential to owning a home and achieving the dreams you have, but it's only as important as the life it helps you live. Buy your biggest asset wisely so you will have money to do all the things you want to do.

And live in your home. Make great art in the garage. Music on the back porch. Paint the dining room shocking pink. Love your wife in it. Love your husband. Love *somebody.* Raise your children in your home. Mark their heights on the kitchen door frame. Ache as you stand in their empty bedrooms after they've left, and fill the place again with grandchildren on holidays. Share Super Bowl Sundays with your pals and welcome the neighbors after a big storm takes off their roof. Have a good time.

Don't let buying your house get in the way of living in your home. Don't shovel money at it, don't feed it and don't let it enslave you. A home shouldn't be a burden. It's a joy.

THE LIFE EXPECTANCIES OF VARIOUS HOME COMPONENTS

This list was compiled by the National Association of Home Builders in 2007. The complete study is available for free at *http://www.nahb.org/generic.aspx?genericContentID=72539*.

Appliances. Appliances are often replaced long before they are worn out because changes in styling, technology and consumer preferences make newer products more desirable. Of the major home appliances, gas ranges have the longest life expectancy, fifteen years. Dryers and refrigerators last about thirteen years. Appliances with the shortest life span are: compactors (six years), dishwashers (nine years) and microwave ovens (nine years).

Cabinetry and storage. Kitchens are becoming larger and more elaborate, and together with the family room, form the "great room." Kitchen cabinets are expected to last up to fifty years, medicine cabinets for twenty-plus years, and garage/

laundry cabinets for one-hundred-plus years. Closet shelves are expected to last for a lifetime.

Concrete and masonry. Chimneys, fireplaces and brick veneers can last a lifetime, and brick walls have an average life expectancy of more than one hundred years.

Countertops. Natural stone countertops are expected to last a lifetime. Cultured marble countertops have a life expectancy of about twenty years.

Decks. Under ideal conditions, they have a life expectancy of about twenty years.

Doors. Exterior fiberglass, steel and wood doors will last as long as the house exists, while vinyl and screen doors have a life expectancy of twenty and forty years, respectively. Closet doors are expected to last a lifetime, and French doors have an average life of thirty to fifty years.

Electrical and lighting. Copper-plated wiring, copper-clad aluminum and bare copper wiring are expected to last a lifetime, whereas electrical accessories and lighting controls are expected to last ten-plus years.

Engineered lumber. Floor and roof trusses and laminated strand lumber are expected to last a lifetime, and engineered trim is expected to last thirty years.

Faucets and fixtures. Kitchen sinks made of modified acrylic will last fifty years, while kitchen faucets will work properly for about fifteen years. The average life of bathroom shower enclosures is fifty years. Showerheads last a lifetime, while shower doors will last about twenty years. Whirlpool tubs will function properly for twenty to fifty years, depending on use. Bath cabinets and toilets have an unlimited life span, but the components inside the toilet tank do require some maintenance.

Flooring. All natural wood floorings have a life expectancy of one hundred years or more. Marble, slate, and granite are also expected to last for about one hundred years but can last less due to a lack of maintenance. Vinyl floors last up to fifty years, linoleum about twenty-five years and carpet between eight and ten years (with appropriate maintenance and normal traffic).

Footings and foundations. Poured as well as concrete block footings and foundations last a lifetime, assuming they were properly built. Termite-proofing of foundations will last about twelve years if the chemical barriers put in place during construction are left intact. Waterproofing with bituminous coating lasts ten years, but if it cracks it is immediately damaged. Concrete or cast-iron waste pipes are expected to last one hundred years or more.

Framing and other structural systems. Poured-concrete systems, timber frame houses and structural insulated panels will all last a lifetime. Wall panels and roof and floor trusses will similarly last a lifetime.

Softwood, hardboard and plywood last an average of thirty years, while oriented strand board (OSB) and particleboard are expected to function properly for sixty years.

Garages. Garage door openers are expected to last ten to fifteen years, and light inserts for twenty years.

Gutters. Fifty years if made of copper and twenty years for aluminum. Copper downspouts last one hundred years or more, while aluminum ones will last thirty years.

Heating, ventilation and air-conditioning. Systems require proper and regular maintenance, but even the best components last only fifteen to twenty-five years. Furnaces on average last fifteen to twenty years, heat pumps sixteen years, and air-conditioning units ten to fifteen years. Tankless water heaters last more than twenty years, while an electric or gas water heater has a life expectancy of about ten years. Thermostats usually are replaced before the end of their thirty-five-year life span.

Home technology. Home technology systems have various life expectancies. While a built-in audio system will last twenty years, security systems and heat/smoke detectors have life expectancies of five to ten years. Wireless home networks and home automation systems are expected to work properly for more than fifty years.

Insulation and infiltration barriers. As long as they are not punctured, cut or burned and are kept dry and away from UV rays, the cellulose, fiberglass and foam used in insulation materials will last a lifetime.

Molding and millwork. Custom millwork and all stairs—circular and spiral, pre-built and attic—are expected to last a lifetime.

Paint, chalks and adhesives. Both interior and exterior paints can last for fifteen years or longer; however, home owners often paint more frequently.

Panels. Hardboard panels and softwood panels are expected to last thirty years, while oriented strand board and particleboard have a life expectancy of twenty-five to thirty years. Wall panels are expected to last a lifetime.

Roofing. The life of a roof depends on local weather conditions, material quality and maintenance. Slate, copper and clay or concrete roofs have the longest life expectancy—more than fifty years. Roofs made of asphalt shingles last for about twenty years; fiber-cement shingles have a life expectancy of about twenty-five years and wood shakes can be expected to last for about thirty years.

Siding and accessories. Outside materials typically last a lifetime. Brick, vinyl, engineered wood, stone (both natural and manufactured) and fiber cement will last as long the house exists. Exterior wood shutters are expected to last twenty years, depending on weather conditions.

Site and landscaping. Most landscaping elements have a life expectancy of fifteen to twenty-five years. Sprinklers and valves last about twenty years, while underground PVC piping has a life span of twenty-five years. An asphalt driveway should last between fifteen and twenty years. Tennis court coatings last twelve to fifteen years. The concrete shell of a swimming pool is expected to last more than twenty-five years, but the interior plaster and tile have life expectancies of about ten to twenty-five years.

Windows and skylights. Aluminum windows are expected to last between fifteen and twenty years while wooden windows should last upward of thirty years.

A Home Owner's Maintenance Checklist

Most home maintenance activities are seasonal. Fall is the time to get your home ready for the coming winter, which can be the most grueling season for your home. During winter months, it is important to follow routine maintenance procedures, by checking your home carefully for any problems arising and taking corrective action as soon as possible. Spring is the time to assess winter damage, start repairs and prepare for warmer months. Over the summer, there are a number of indoor and outdoor maintenance tasks to look after, such as repairing walkways and steps, painting and checking your chimney and roof.

While most maintenance is seasonal, there are some things you should do on a frequent basis year-round. The following checklist is adapted from the Canada Mortgage and Housing Corporation, a government agency:

- Make sure air vents indoors and outdoors (intake, exhaust and forced air) are not blocked by snow or debris.

- Check and clean range hood filters on a monthly basis.

- Test the ground fault circuit interrupter(s) monthly by pushing the test button, which should then cause the reset button to pop up.

- If there are young children in the house, make sure electrical outlets are equipped with safety plugs.

- Regularly check the house for safety hazards such as a loose handrail, lifting or buckling carpet, etc.

FALL

- Have the furnace or heating system serviced by a qualified service company every two years for a gas furnace and every year for an oil furnace.

- Open the furnace humidifier damper on units with central air-conditioning and clean the humidifier.

- Lubricate the circulating pump on your hot water heating system.

- Bleed air from hot water radiators.

- Examine the forced air furnace fan belt for wear, looseness or noise; clean fan blades of any dirt buildup (after disconnecting the electricity to the motor first).

- Turn on the gas furnace pilot light.

- Check and clean or replace furnace air filters each month during the heating season. Ventilation system, such as heat recovery ventilator, filters should be checked every two months.

- Vacuum electric baseboard heaters to remove dust.

- Remove the grills on forced air systems and vacuum inside the ducts.

- If the heat recovery ventilator has been shut off for the summer, clean the filters and the core, and pour water down the condensate drain to test it.

- Clean the portable humidifier, if one is used.

- Have well water tested for quality. It is recommended that you test for bacteria every six months.

- Check sump pump and line to ensure proper operation and to ascertain that there are no line obstructions or visible leaks.

- Replace window screens with storm windows.

- Remove screens from the inside of casement windows to allow air from the heating system to keep condensation off window glass.

- Ensure all doors to the outside shut tightly and check other doors for ease of use. Renew door weather stripping if required.

- If there is a door between your house and the garage, check the adjustment of the self-closing device to ensure it closes the door completely.

- Ensure windows and skylights close tightly.

- Cover the outside of air-conditioning units.

- Ensure that the ground around your home slopes away from the foundation wall so that water does not drain into your basement.

- Clean leaves from the eaves, gutters and roof, and test downspouts to ensure proper drainage from the roof.

- Check chimneys for obstructions such as nests.

- Drain and store outdoor hoses. Close the valve to the outdoor hose connection and drain the hose bib (exterior faucet), unless your house has frost-proof hose bibs.

- If you have a septic tank, measure the sludge and scum to determine if the tank needs to be emptied before the spring. Tanks should be pumped out at least once every three years.

- Winterize landscaping. For example, store outdoor furniture, prepare gardens and, if necessary, protect young trees or bushes for winter.

WINTER

- Check and clean or replace furnace air filters each month during the heating season. Ventilation system, such as heat recovery ventilator and filters, should be checked every two months.

- After consulting your hot water tank owner's manual, drain off a dishpan full of water from the clean-out valve at the bottom of your hot water tank to control sediment and maintain efficiency.

- Clean the humidifier two or three times during the winter season.

- Vacuum the bathroom fan grill.

- Vacuum fire and smoke detectors, as dust or spider-webs can prevent them from functioning.

- Vacuum radiator grills on the back of refrigerators and freezers, and empty and clean drip trays.

- Check the gauge on all fire extinguishers; recharge or replace if necessary.

- Check fire escape routes, door and window locks and hardware, and lighting around the outside of the house; ensure family has good security habits.

- Check the basement floor drain to ensure the trap contains water. Refill with water if necessary.

- Monitor your home for excessive moisture levels— for example, condensation on your windows, which can cause significant damage over time and pose serious health problems—and take corrective action.

- Check all faucets for signs of dripping and change washers as needed. Faucets requiring frequent replacement of washers may be in need of repair.

- If you have a plumbing fixture that is not used frequently, such as a laundry tub or spare bathroom sink, tub or shower stall, run some water briefly to keep water in the trap.

- Clean drains in the dishwasher, sinks, bathtubs and shower stalls.

- Test shut-off valves on plumbing to ensure they are working and to prevent them from seizing.

- Examine windows and doors for ice accumulation or cold air leaks. If found, make a note to repair or replace in the spring.

- Examine attic for frost accumulation. Check roof for ice dams or icicles.

- Check electrical cords, plugs and outlets for all indoor and outdoor seasonal lights to ensure fire safety: if worn, or if plugs or cords feel warm to the touch, replace immediately.

SPRING

- After consulting your hot water tank owner's manual, carefully test the temperature and pressure relief valve to ensure it is not stuck. Caution: This test may release hot water that can cause burns. Be careful.

- Check and clean or replace furnace air filters each month during the heating season. Ventilation system, such as heat recovery ventilator, filters should be checked every two months.

- Have fireplace or woodstove and chimney cleaned and serviced as needed.

- Shut down and clean furnace humidifier, and close the furnace humidifier damper on units with central air-conditioning.

- Check air-conditioning system and have it serviced every two or three years.

- Clean or replace air-conditioning filter (if applicable).

- Check dehumidifier and clean if necessary.

- Turn off gas furnace and fireplace pilot lights where possible.

- Have well water tested for quality. It is recommended that you test for bacteria every six months.

- Check smoke, carbon monoxide and security alarms and replace batteries.

- Clean windows, screens and hardware, and replace storm windows with screens. Check screens first and repair or replace if needed.

- Open valve to outside hose connection after all danger of frost has passed.

- Examine the foundation walls for cracks, leaks or signs of moisture, and repair as required. Repair and paint fences as necessary.

- Ensure sump pump is operating properly before the spring thaw sets in. Ensure discharge pipe is connected and allows water to drain away from the foundation.

- Re-level any exterior steps or decks that moved due to frost or settling.

- Check eaves, gutters and downspouts for loose joints and secure attachment to your home, clear any obstructions, and ensure water flows away from your foundation.

- Clear all drainage ditches and culverts of debris.

- Undertake spring landscape maintenance and, if necessary, fertilize young trees.

SUMMER

- Monitor basement humidity and avoid relative humidity levels above 60 percent. Use a dehumidifier to maintain a safe relative humidity. Clean or replace the air-conditioning filter, and wash or replace ventilation system filters if necessary.

- Check basement pipes for condensation or dripping, and take corrective action. For example, reduce humidity and/or insulate cold water pipes.

- Check the basement floor drain to ensure the trap contains water. Refill with water if necessary.

- If you have a plumbing fixture that is not used frequently, for example, a laundry tub or spare bathroom sink, tub or shower stall, run some water briefly to keep water in the trap.

- Deep clean carpets and rugs.

- Vacuum bathroom fan grill.

- Disconnect the duct connected to the dryer and vacuum lint from the duct, the areas surrounding your clothes dryer and your dryer's vent hood outside.

- Check security of all guardrails and handrails.

- Check smooth functioning of all windows and lubricate as required.

- Inspect window putty on outside of glass panes and replace if needed.

- Lubricate door hinges and tighten screws as needed.

- Lubricate garage door hardware and ensure it is operating properly.

- Lubricate automatic garage door opener motor, chain and so forth and ensure that the auto-reverse mechanism is properly adjusted.

- Check and replace damaged caulking and weather stripping around windows and doorways, including the doorway between the garage and the house.

- Inspect electrical service lines for secure attachment where they enter your house, and make sure there is no water leakage into the house along the electrical conduit.

- Check exterior wood siding and trim for signs of deterioration; clean, replace or refinish as needed.

- Check for and seal off any holes in exterior cladding that could be an entry point for small pests, such as bats and squirrels.

- Remove any plants that contact, or roots that penetrate, the siding or brick.

- Climb up on your roof, or use binoculars, to check its general condition, and note any sagging that could indicate structural problems requiring further investigation from inside the attic. Note the condition of all shingles for possible repair or replacement, and examine all roof flashings, such as at chimney and roof joints, for any signs of cracking or leakage.

- Sweep chimneys connected to any wood-burning appliance or fireplace, and inspect them for end-of-season problems.

Check the chimney cap and the caulking between the cap and the chimney.

- Repair driveway and walkways as needed.

- Repair any damaged steps that present a safety problem.

GLOSSARY

HOME TALK:
TERMS AND CONCEPTS
OF HOME OWNING

If much of the language of real estate has a medieval flavor to it, that's because real-estate practices in the United States trace back to William the Conqueror's invasion of England in 1066. When William took over, he claimed all the new land for himself—the *real* in *real estate* actually derives from *royal* so *real estate* means "royal ownership of the property." William then gave grants, titles or deeds to his Norman pals and to the local nobles who welcomed him. (You can imagine what happened to properties of the locals who weren't so welcoming.)

Because land cannot be pocketed like gold or herded like cattle, the king and the landlords had to come up with a way of registering property boundaries and recording ownership. The landlords had to know where their tenants could farm, cut wood or graze livestock. And the king needed to know how much his sheriff could collect in taxes from the yeomanry and the property owners. (Yes, this is what the Robin Hood story is all about.)

Today, every county courthouse in the country maintains property records of all the land in the county. Anyone can consult the county maps to learn the boundaries and ownership of every lot of real estate in the county and who has filed liens or claims for money against them. In most U.S. counties, it's still the sheriff who is charged with carrying out real-estate-related actions, such as foreclosures, auctions and evictions.

The Normans would recognize our system, but they—and you—might need some help with a few modern terms.

Adjusted cost basis. For tax purposes, the cost of the house (excluding operating expenses and interest) that is used to determine your profit or loss when you sell your house. Cost basis is calculated by adding the amount you paid for the house to how much you spent on capital improvements and subtracting any capital losses. Capital improvements are renovations that increase a home's value, such as enlarging a kitchen or adding a bedroom. An example of a loss would be repair of fire or storm damage not reimbursed by insurance.

Annual percentage rate (APR). The actual cost of borrowing money. It will be higher than the quoted interest rate because it includes the interest rate, loan origination fees, loan discount points and other credit costs.

Appraisal. An estimate of a property's fair market value. It is typically based on estimates of replacement cost, income or, for most single-family homes, comparable sales of similar properties.

Appreciation. Increase in the value of a property based on overall market inflation.

ARM. An adjustable rate mortgage is a loan subject to changes in interest rates; when rates change, ARM monthly payments increase or decrease at intervals determined by the lender.

Assumable mortgage. Rare in residential real estate, but not necessarily out of the question in a troubled housing market. An assumable mortgage allows the next purchaser of a property to carry on the payments and other obligations of an existing note and mortgage.

Balloon loan. Also called a "bullet loan," a balloon loan is amortized over a long period but must be paid in a shorter one, typically resulting in a large final payment due at the end of the loan period. Example: if a note is written for $200,000 at a fixed 6.5% rate of interest with payments based on an amortization schedule of thirty years and a balloon payment due in five years, the first fifty-nine payments will each be $1,264, and the last payment will be $187,000.

Bridge loan. A temporary loan that buyers often use to acquire a property quickly. Most often, buyers use bridge loans to buy a new property while another is being sold.

Cap. The limit on how much the interest rate or monthly payment on an adjustable rate mortgage (ARM) can go up or down. There are three types of caps: First, lifetime caps set the top limit that a lender can charge—a 12% lifetime cap, for example, means the interest rate can never go above 12%—second, the first adjustment cap limits the rate change on the ARM's initial adjustment; and third, periodic caps limit the rate changes on the following adjustment periods.

Closing. Also known as settlement, this is the time at which the property is formally sold and transferred from the seller to the buyer. Sellers rarely show up at closings. If you are the buyer, you sign a lot of papers and, for a moment, you might hold a really, really big check for the total of the mortgage. In some states, closings are conducted by attorneys. Elsewhere they are handled by escrow agents.

Closing costs. Various outrageous, inexplicable fees and expenses payable by the seller or buyer at the time of a real-estate closing, including but rarely limited to broker commissions, title insurance, lender fees, recording fees, inspection fees, appraisal fees and attorney's fees.

Community property. What's mine is mine; what's yours is yours and what's ours is half mine and half yours. Property that is jointly owned by a married husband and wife. This applies only in states with community-property laws, where each spouse owns one-half of the property bought during their marriage. In general, both spouses have equal control over how the property is managed, and if one spouse wants to hand over his or her interest to someone else, the other must agree. Also, either spouse can will his or her share to anyone he or she wants.

Comparable sales. Recent sales of similar properties, to determine the fair-market value of a property. "Comps," as they are sometimes called, should have as many similarities as possible, including neighborhood, square footage, lot size, construction, room count, floor plan, amenities and traffic patterns.

Condominium. A form of home ownership in which individuals buy apartments in a multi-unit complex. The "condo" owners share financial responsibility for common areas.

Conforming loan. A loan that conforms to the underwriting guidelines of Fannie Mae (Federal National Mortgage Association), Freddie Mac (Federal Home Loan Mortgage Corporation), the Federal Housing Administration or the Department of Veterans Affairs. In 2008, the conforming loan limit for a single-family property was redefined to 115% of the local median house price, up to $625,000. There are other, higher conforming-loan limits for multi-family properties.

Loans for amounts greater than the conforming limits usually carry a slightly higher interest rate and are called "jumbo loans."

Cooperative (co-op). Similar—but different—from a condominium. Limited mainly to New York, Washington, Chicago and a few other cities, co-op residents purchase stock in a cooperative corporation that owns an apartment building. Each stockholder is then entitled to live in a specific apartment as a tenant. Shareholders are responsible for all expenses, including debts, of the corporation.

Debt-to-income ratio. A lender's gauge of a borrower's ability to make the monthly payments on a loan, based on the percentage of a borrower's monthly pre-tax income that goes to debt payments.

Lenders typically prefer that borrowers spend no more than 28% of their monthly income for housing and 8% more on all other debts, but ratios can vary according to the credit-worthiness of the borrower and local custom. In high-cost areas, lenders are more likely to allow a higher percentage of income for housing, as much as 40% in places such as New York or San Francisco.

Prudent practice: keep your total housing cost to no more than 25% of your pretax income.

Deed in lieu of foreclosure. A deed surrendered by a borrower to a lender to satisfy a mortgage debt and avoid foreclosure.

Deed of trust. A legal feint used in many states in place of a mortgage. While a mortgage is between a borrower and lender, a deed of trust involves a borrower, a lender and a trustee, who holds the property in trust as security for the debt. A deed of trust makes it easier to foreclose on a home buyer in default.

Discount points. The good kind of points. Interest paid "up front," at the time that a loan is funded, mainly to lower the note rate of the loan and the monthly payment.

Example: A "no points" $200,000 loan at 6.5% for thirty

years costs $1,264 a month. If, however, you were willing to pay four points (4%, or $8,000) up front, you could get $200,000 for just 5.5% and save $128 a month. In this case, the extra up-front cost will be paid back in about sixty-two months, so you would come out ahead if you own the property for five years.

In contrast, if you use the $8,000 to make a larger down payment and, thus a lower beginning balance, you'll save $50 a month for thirty years but pay about $36,000 more in interest due to the higher rate. If you buy $8,000 worth of Treasury bonds, your annual income will be just $336. Best scenario? Pay the discount points and use the $128 to make an additional principal payment each month. You'll pay off the mortgage about six years early and save $97,000 in interest.

Earnest money. A good-faith deposit made when you are buying a house. Local practices and preferred amounts vary. In some places you are expected to include an earnest money check with a written offer; in others you put up your earnest money after an oral offer has been accepted and a contract has been written.

Energy Efficient Mortgage. A federal program administered by the Federal Housing Administration that allows home buyers to finance the cost of adding energy-efficient features to a new or existing home as part of the home purchase.

Equity. A home owner's actual ownership interest in a property, measured as the difference between the market value and the principal mortgage balance and any other liens or debts secured by the house.

Escrow account. A separate account into which the lender puts a portion of each monthly mortgage payment. An escrow account provides the funds needed for such expenses as property taxes or home-owners insurance that are paid throughout the year.

Fee simple. A "fee simple estate" is the most common form of land ownership in the United States. It means the owner's interest is total, and his land rights include the right to sell the property or pass it to heirs. Other forms of ownership, though quite rare among single-family houses, include a "life estate" where the previous owner retakes possession upon the life-estate owner's death, or an "estate for years," in which ownership lasts for only a fixed time. Similar to that and more common in the United States is a leasehold estate, which can last for decades (ninety-nine-year leaseholds are quite common).

Foreclosure. A procedure by which a lender ("mortgagee") takes title or forces the sale of a borrower's ("mortgagor") property. It's always good to avoid a foreclosure.

And be careful. It's rare, but the IRS can come looking for money after the lender takes over your property. The government can view the wiping out of the loan as what it likes to call a "taxable event." Here's the thinking: if you default on a $100,000 loan, and the lender then sells the property for $80,000, in the eyes of the IRS, you have been forgiven $20,000 of debt. That's income. Uh-oh.

Index. The cost of money that is used to determine the interest rate for an adjustable rate mortgage (ARM). Common indexes (all are published daily in *The Wall Street Journal*) are: the prime rate, the London Interbank Offered Rate (LIBOR), the Cost of Funds (COF) and the one-year Treasury bill.

Generally, loans that adjust monthly use the prime rate; loans that adjust semi-annually use LIBOR, and loans that adjust annually use the Treasury bill or the Cost of Funds. Typically, a margin of about two percentage points is added to the index to set the mortgage rate. So, if the one-year Treasury bill is yielding 4.26%, an ARM pegged to it would carry a rate of about 6.26%.

Initial-adjustment period. The term on an adjustable-rate mortgage (ARM) when the lowest "initial interest rate" is in effect. After that, the rate adjusts to reflect prevailing market interest rates.

Joint tenancy and tenants in common. Two ways to take title of a property by two or more persons. In a joint tenancy, each owner has an "undivided" interest. Outside community-property states, married couples and domestic partners usually hold properties as joint tenants, so that either spouse or partner will own the property completely when the other dies. Unrelated partners, however, are far more likely to own properties as tenants in common, with each partner owning just a portion that is passed on to an estate upon the partner's death. During the bubble era, it became common in some big cities for unrelated property buyers to acquire houses as tenants in common.

Lease option. A lease that combines a rental agreement with an option agreement that gives the lessee (tenant) the right to purchase the property in the future. A lease option will usually require some additional monthly or annual payment to keep the option in effect.

Lease purchase. More common in down markets when homes are hard to sell, a lease purchase agreement combines renting with buying. A tenant will usually pay a fixed amount over the monthly rent that will, over time, add up to a down payment.

Loan officer. Employee at a loan company who works with individuals to identify and explain the various loan products available to mortgage borrowers. The loan officer typically conducts the initial review of the mortgage application.

Loan-to-value ratio (LTV). Loan principal divided by the property's appraised value. Typical home loans have a loan-to-value of 80% or 90%, although during the bubble era, 100% loans were common.

Mortgage. French for "dead pledge," a written promise to pay back a loan secured by real estate. Most mortgages are written for thirty-year payback or "amortization" periods that require hefty interest payments early in the period and gradually increasing principal payments.

The government subsidizes home mortgage costs via the interest-payment deduction in the income-tax code. Regardless, over the entire length of a thirty-year mortgage, interest payments will far outstrip principal payments, so it is always best for a borrower who plans to hold property for a long time to pay off a mortgage ahead of schedule.

Properties can have multiple mortgages. The principal or senior mortgage on a property is the first mortgage. That's what most home owners have. A home-equity loan or line of credit is a subordinate, usually a second mortgage. After the government, the holder of the first mortgage has the first claim on a property in any default. Subordinate mortgages are labeled according to the date of recording as second, third, and so on.

Mortgage broker. A company that, for a commission, matches borrowers and lenders. A mortgage broker typically takes the borrower application and sometimes processes the loan but, unlike a mortgage banker, does not use its own funds to close the loan.

Mortgage modification. A step that may be taken in the period before a foreclosure (or a refinance), in which the borrower and the lender agree to change the terms of the existing mortgage loan, primarily to reduce the monthly payments.

Negative amortization. A very bad consequence of taking out an adjustable-rate mortgage that features exceptionally low interest rates. If a borrower makes just the minimum payment, it may not cover all of the interest that would normally be due. The difference, which is called "deferred interest," is then added to the principal so the balance on the loan grows larger instead of smaller. In a declining real-estate market, this can be devastating as a property owner could end up owing far more on a loan than the property is worth.

Negative equity. Condition achieved when the market value of a property declines by more than the borrower's equity position—that is, the sum of the original down payment, any loan principal repayments and house-price appreciation. For example, suppose a borrower puts down $20,000 to buy a home, and the value of the property promptly declines by more than $25,000. The negative equity amounts to $5,000, meaning the borrower would have to pay $5,000 out-of-pocket to immediately refinance.

Origination fee. Sometimes called "origination points," this is a fee for originating a loan, usually calculated and paid at closing. These are the bad kind of points. You should avoid lenders who insist on these.

PITI. The shorthand way of stating the most usual elements of a residential mortgage payment: Principal, Interest, Taxes and Insurance. When all four are part of the monthly payment, the lender escrows the taxes and insurance and pays them when they come due. (See escrow account.)

PMI. Private mortgage insurance is required on loans with down payments of less than 20% of the purchase price. It protects the interest of lenders, not property owners, in the event of a mortgage default.

Pre-approval (mortgage). When a lender commits to lend to a potential borrower, in contrast to a "pre-qualify," which is an informal determination of the maximum amount you may borrow.

Pre-foreclosure sale. Allows a defaulting borrower to sell a mortgaged property to satisfy the loan and avoid foreclosure.

Quitclaim deed. A short-form deed that passes title to a property, but there is no assurance that the title is valid. Quitclaim deeds frequently are used in divorces to transfer one spouse's property interests to the other. They are also used in real-estate scams, however, to fraudulently convey ownership rights that don't exist.

Real property. The land and anything permanently attached to it such as a house, a driveway or an in-ground swimming pool. In the United States, we make a distinction between realty or immobile property and personal property—your house versus your car, for example. The latter is also called chattel or moveable property.

Refinancing. Paying off one loan with another became the national pastime in the first few years of the century, when interest rates hit forty-year lows and real-estate prices hit all-time highs.

The result? Hocking the house. "Cash-out" refinancing, in which an owner takes advantage of a property's appreciation, refinances for more money than the previous loan and pockets the difference. When home owners try this, however, they are saddled with higher monthly payments and new long-term loan commitments. If they use the extra money to invest, they may be OK. But too many home owners use refinancing proceeds for vacations, cars or other purchases—which they will spend the next thirty years paying for.

Rehab. House flipping. Buy it cheap. Clean it up, fix it up, paint it up. Sell it.

REO (real-estate owned). Residential property acquired by a bank or other mortgage holder, usually through a foreclosure, that is offered for sale. Most large banks have **REO** departments that hold and manage their portfolio of foreclosed properties.

Sale-leaseback. One way for a home owner to take money out of his or her house without moving. In a leaseback deal, an owner-occupant sells property to an investor. The investor-owner (who could be a grown child) agrees to lease the property back to the previous owner, who will then continue to live in the house as a tenant.

Short sale. Selling a house for less than its mortgage amount. A special type of pre-foreclosure sale, a short sale usually takes place after a home owner has defaulted on his house but before formal foreclosure. The lender must approve the terms of the sale. It is generally less advantageous for the buyer to buy in a short sale from the owner than to wait until the foreclosure is complete and the bank takes control of the property.

Tax liens and tax deeds. A tax lien is a claim on a property, usually by a state or local government, for delinquent property taxes. All mortgages and other liens are subordinate to a tax lien. That means the government's claim on a property comes before even the holder of the first mortgage and even if the mortgage debt is far greater than the amount of the back taxes. (A tax deed is issued when the government actually seizes a property.)

In most tax-lien states, third parties can buy the liens at auction for just the cost of the back taxes and penalties. That transfers the government's claim on the property to the investor. If the property owner fails to retire the tax lien, the investor can take the property. Redemption time periods vary greatly by state—usually from one to five years. And some states even allow delinquent owners to redeem their property after a tax-deed sale. The IRS also acquires and sells properties for unpaid taxes.

TYPES OF HOME CONSTRUCTION

Manufactured housing. A trailer. Housing structures built in accordance with the Department of Housing and Urban Development (HUD) code. Unlike other forms of housing built to a state or local construction code, manufactured-housing units must have an integral chassis and must be transported on their own axles and wheels in one or more sections from the factory.

Mobile home. An older trailer. Manufactured-housing unit that either was built before 1976 or does not comply with the HUD code. Modular housing. Residential structures built in sections in a factory and then transported by trailer to homesites, where they are lifted onto foundations and permanently anchored.

Panelized housing. Residential structures built from wall panels assembled at the factory and then transported to the construction site.

Site-built housing. Residential structures built to state or local construction standards that are constructed (stick built) or assembled (modular or panelized) at the property site.

Title insurance. Like private mortgage insurance, title insurance is a protection for lenders that home owners pay for. Title companies issue expensive policies insuring against loss resulting from defects of title or claims or liens related to a specific property. Lenders usually require a new title-insurance policy each time a property changes hands or is refinanced.

Workout. Mutual agreement between a lender and borrower who is behind on his mortgage payments. A workout is a type of mortgage modification, which usually entails deferring principal payments, additional interest or some other arrangement that results in extending the term of the mortgage.

BIBLIOGRAPHY

This list of books and Web sites is not meant to be exhaustive. Along with the sources cited in the text, these are the published materials that I most frequently visited to check facts, figures and insights.

There are scores of very good, useful sources that I have failed to include and hundreds, if not thousands, of not so good ones that I haven't listed, either. I have arranged these in a Good-Better-Best arrangement to give you some idea of what I found to be most useful for this presentation.

I appreciate the time, energy and effort that these authors have put into their works, and I acknowledge the help that each and every one of them has given me.

BOOKS

BEST

Bray, Ilona; Schroeder, Alayna; Stewart, Marcia. *Nolo's Essential Guide to Buying Your First Home.* Nolo Press, 2007.

Crook, David. *The Wall Street Journal. Complete Real-Estate Investing Guidebook.* Three Rivers Press, 2006.

Elred, Gary W. *The 106 Common Mistakes Homebuyers Make,* 4th Edition. John Wiley & Sons, 2006.

Exterior Home Improvement Costs, 9th Edition. RS Means/Reed Construction Data, 2004.

Garton-Good, Julie. *The Frugal Home Owner's Guide to Buying, Selling & Improving Your Home.* Dearborn Trade Publishing, 1999.

Glink, Ilyce R. *10 Steps to Home Ownership.* Times Books/Random House, 1996.

Interior Home Improvement Costs, 9th Edition. RS Means/Reed Construction Data, 2004.

Kiplinger's Buying and Selling a Home, 8th Edition. Kaplan Publishing, 2006.

Means Residential Square Foot Costs: Contractor's Pricing Guide 2008. RS Means/Reed Construction Data, 2007.

Miller, Peter G. *The Common-Sense Mortgage.* Contemporary Books, 1999.

O'Hara, Shelley and Lewis, Nancy D. *The Complete Idiot's Guide to Buying & Selling a Home,* 5th Edition. Alpha Books/Penguin, 2006.

Opdyke, Jeff. *The Wall Street Journal. Complete Personal Finance Guidebook.* Three Rivers Press, 2006.

Robinson, Gerald J. *J. K. Lasser's Homeowner's Tax Breaks.* John Wiley & Sons, 2004.

Ruffenach, Glenn and Greene, Kelly. *The Wall Street Journal. Complete Retirement Guidebook.* Three Rivers Press, 2007.

Tyson, Eric and Brow, Ray. *Home Buying for Dummies,* 3rd Edition. Wiley Publishing, 2006.

Wilson, Alex; Thorne, Jennifer; Morrill, John. *Consumer Guide to Home Energy Savings,* 8th Edition. American Council for an Energy-Efficient Economy, 2003.

Better

Bach, David. *The Automatic Millionaire Homeowner.* Broadway Books, 2005.

Cummins, Joseph Eamon. *Not One Dollar More!* 2nd Edition. John Wiley & Sons, 1999.

Daum, Kevin; Brewster, Janice; and Economy, Peter. *Building Your Own Home for Dummies.* Wiley Publishing, 2005.

Fletcher, June. *House Poor.* Collins, 2005.

Holton, Lisa. *The Essential Dictionary of Real Estate.* Barnes & Noble Books, 2004.

Irwin, Robert. *Buy Right, Sell High.* Real Estate Education Co./Dearborn, 1997.

Lyons, Sarah Glendon and Lucas, John E. *Reverse Mortgage for Dummies.* Wiley Publishing, 2005.

National Association of Realtors Guide to Home Buying. John Wiley & Sons, 2007.

National Association of Realtors Guide to Home Selling. John Wiley & Sons, 2007.

Paxton, Albert S. *2008 National Repair & Remodeling Estimator.* Craftsman Book Company, 2007.

Talbott, John. *The Coming Crash in the Housing Market.* McGraw-Hill, 2003.

Thomsett, Michael C. and Kahr, Joshua. *Beyond the Bubble.* Amacom, 2007.

Vitt, Lois A. *10 Secrets to Successful Home Buying and Selling.* Pearson/Prentice-Hall, 2005.

Willis, Gerri. *Home Rich.* Ballantine Books, 2008.

GOOD

Clark, Teri B. *301 Simple Things You Can Do to Sell Your Home Now . . .* Atlantic Publishing Group, 2007.

Davis, Sid. *Home Makeovers that Sell.* Amacom, 2007.

De Heer, Robert. *Realty Bluebook,* 33rd Edition. Dearborn Real Estate Education, 2003.

Eilers, Terry. *How to Buy the Home You Want for the Best Price in Any Market.* Hyperion, 1997.

H & R Block Just Plain Smart Home Buying Advisor. Random House Reference, 2004.

Levy, Michael A. *Home Ownership: The American Myth,* 2nd Edition. Myth Breakers, 1993.

Papolos, Janice. *The Virgin Homeowner.* Penguin Books, 1997.

Reed, David. *Mortgage Confidential.* Amacom, 2007.

Roth, Julian (ed.). *How to Buy or Build a Home of Your Own.* Wise & Co./Greystone Press, 1947.

Sumichrast, Michael; Shafer, Ronald G.; Sumichrast, Martin A. *The New Complete Book of Home Buying.* McGraw-Hill, 2005.

Thrift and Home Ownership: Your Safeguards for Freedom. California Savings & Loan League, 1959.

WEB SITES

BEST

American Council for an Energy-Efficient Economy: *http://www.aceee.org*

Bankrate.com: *http://www.bankrate.com*

Department of Housing and Urban Development: *http://www.hud.gov*

Dinkytown: *http://www.dinkytown.net*
Energy Star: *http://www.energystar.gov/*
Fannie Mae: *http://www.fanniemae.com*
Freddie Mac: *http://www.freddiemac.com*
Internal Revenue Service: *http://www.irs.gov*
Mortgage Professor: *http://www.mtgprofessor.com*
National Association of Realtors: *http://www.realtor.org*
NOLO Press: *http://www.nolo.com*
Real Estate Journal *(The Wall Street Journal): http://www.realestatejournal.com*

BETTER

Andy Sirkin, attorney: *http://andysirkin.com*
Building-Cost.net: *http://www.building-cost.net*
Canada Mortgage and Housing Corp.: *http://www.cmhc-schl.gc.ca/en/co/*
Economics and Statistics Administration (Department of Commerce):
　https:// www.esa.doc.gov
Home Pages: *http://www.homepages.com*
Ilyce Glink: *http://www.thinkglink.com*
Inman News: *http://www.inman.com*
Investopedia: *http://www.investopedia.com*
Money magazine real estate: *http://money.cnn.com/real_estate*
Mortgage 101: *http://www.mortgage101.com*
National Association of Home Builders: *http://www.nahb.org*
RS Means (Reed Construction Data): *http://www.rsmeans.com*

GOOD

Appraisal Institute: *http://appraisalinstitute.org/*
HSH Associates Financial Publishers: *http://www.hsh.com*
Loan Modification and Home Loan News: *http://loanworkout.org/*
National Association of Exclusive Buyer Agents: *http://www.naeba.org/*
National Reverse Mortgage Lenders Association: *http://www.reverse
　mortgage.org/*
Real Estate Tax Issues for Homeowners: *http://www.real-estate-owner.com*

ACKNOWLEDGMENTS

In addition to all the persons named in the book who shared their time and stories, *The Wall Street Journal. Complete Home Owner's Guidebook* could not have been written without the help of dozens of others.

Kelly K. Spors, a reporter and columnist for *The Wall Street Journal,* contributed interviews, research and fact-checking to this project. Her contributions to the book are on every page.

The staff of *The Wall Street Journal Sunday:* Jaclyne Badal, Shelly Banjo, Richard Breeden, Dan Clark, Karen Damato, Emily Green, Diana Ransom, Mark Tyner and others ably managed when I was buried in the manuscript at home. And thanks, too, to business-side associates Paul Bell, Steven Townsley, Mark Pope and Matt Goldberg, and to our production team, including Chris Kunz, Bill Yorke and Tom Post. I also want to single out a former Sunday *Journal* staffer, designer Kristen Girard, whose question three years ago about buying a first home focused me on this project.

My boss, Larry Rout, and news editor John Leger recognized that my previous book, *The Wall Street Journal. Complete Real-Estate Investing Guidebook,* had within it the germ of this one. They encouraged me with an assignment for the paper that eventually transformed into the first chapter of this book.

At WSJ Books: No thank-you is special enough for Roe D'Angelo, who early on seemed to be the only other person in the building who wanted to see this book written and published.

Additional thanks to Alan Murray, to colleague (and nephew) Marshall Crook and to Jim Pensiero and Ken Wells. At Crown: Lindsay Orman and John Mahaney.

Elsewhere at Dow Jones: A number of individuals—from Peter Kann to Rupert Murdoch, from Paul Steiger to Robert Thomson—steered us through a challenging time for our paper and our parent company. None contributed directly to this effort, but they all have made it possible by building and preserving a special enterprise and a great community of journalists.

Also: Pam Abrahamsson, Greg Askins, Bronwyn Belling, Ben Buck, Raoul Burchette, Mitch Capor, Rachel Carpenter, Jonathan Clements, Andrew Coleman, Leonard and Karen Crook, Roger Cruzman, Phil Danner, Karl Ebert, John Erikson, Paul Ferrell, Will Galway, Harold M. George, Ilyce Glink, Dan Gross, Doug Guillaume, Jesse Haifley, Bob Hansen, Amy Hoak, Brad Inman, David Cay Johnston, Steve Kerch, Harlan Landes, David Leen, Debra Lumpkins, June Mathis, Bill McBride, Dennis McDougal, Dave Nathan, Karen Pensiero, Leonard and Barbara Russo, Nick Saines, Ed Sallee, Ruth Simon and Robert Toth.

Finally: Jamie and Lauren. World enough and time.

INDEX

ABOUT THE AUTHOR

DAVID CROOK is the editor of *The Wall Street Journal Sunday* and author of *The Wall Street Journal. Complete Real-Estate Investing Guidebook.*

Sunday Journal is the eight million circulation personal-finance section that appears in more than seventy newspapers around the country. He designed and launched *WSJ Sunday* in 1999, after working on the original team that developed and started the successful "Weekend Journal" section of the daily *Wall Street Journal.* Prior to that, David developed "Home Front" and "Property Report," the paper's residential and commercial real-estate sections.

Before he joined the *Journal* in 1995, David was a reporter and editor at the *Los Angeles Times* and managing editor of a chain of suburban newspapers in southern California. He and his family own a co-op apartment in New York City and a farmhouse built in 1780 in rural Connecticut.

GET YOUR FINANCIAL LIFE IN ORDER WITH THE MOST TRUSTED NAME IN THE WORLD OF FINANCE.

Up-to-date and expertly written, *The Wall Street Journal. Complete Money and Investing Guidebook* provides investors with a simple—but not simplistic—grounding in the world of finance.

The Wall Street Journal. Complete Money and Investing Guidebook

978-0-307-23699-9, $14.95 paper (Canada: $21.00)

The Wall Street Journal. Complete Real-Estate Investing Guidebook is the conservative, thoughtful, thrifty investor's guide to building a real-estate empire.

The Wall Street Journal. Complete Real-Estate Investing Guidebook

978-0-307-34562-2, $14.95 paper (Canada: $21.00)

In *The Wall Street Journal. Complete Retirement Guidebook,* you'll learn how to tailor a financial plan for a retirement that could very well be the best part of your life.

The Wall Street Journal. Complete Retirement Guidebook

978-0-307-35099-2, $14.95 paper (Canada: $19.95)

This hands-on, interactive guide to managing your personal finances makes it quick and easy to get your financial life in order and ultimately build wealth.

The Wall Street Journal. Personal Finance Workbook

978-0-307-33601-9, $13.95 paper (Canada: $21.00)